1 9 5 5

ELVIS
ON THE ROAD TO
STARDOM

1 9 5 6

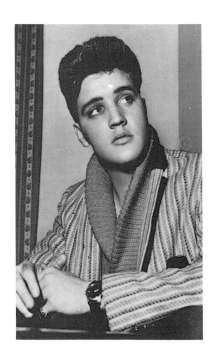

1 9 5 5

ELVIS

ON THE ROAD TO

STARDOM

1 9 5 6

JIM BLACK

W H ALLEN
PLANET

"Down in Tupelo, Mississippi

where I was born, I used to hear old

Arthur Crudup bang his box the

way I do now, and I said if I ever

got to the place I could feel all old

Arthur felt, I'd be a music man like

nobody ever saw."

ELVIS PRESLEY, 1956

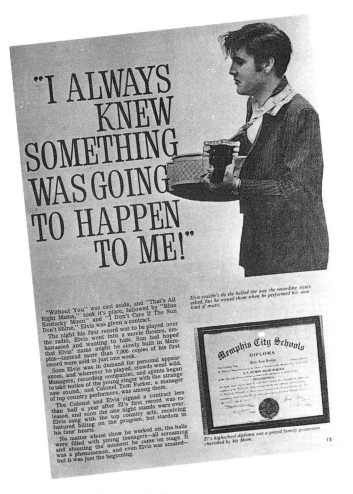

Copyright © Jim Black, 1988

Set in Melior by Phoenix Photosetting
Printed and bound in Spain by Cronion S.A., Barcelona
for the Publishers W.H. Allen & Co Plc
44 Hill Street, London W1X 8LB

ISBN 1–85227–016–0

Front cover illustration by Mickey Shrubsall
Designed by Osborn & Stephens

"Elvis on the road to stardom" – a reconstruction of the singer's early days with Scotty Moore (*right*) and Bill Black for his second film, *Loving You* (1957).

1 the hillbilly cat

It was a moment when one of a young man's most cherished dreams came true. For here he was standing in Basin Street, New Orleans, birthplace of the Blues, which had been an inspiration to him ever since he had been old enough to appreciate the particular kinds of music that were sung and played in this part of America.

The evening was a typical one for a day early in the year, the temperature just below 50 degrees, and the old French-style capital city of the Deep South beside the muddy waters of the Mississippi was alive with the sounds of the two-month-long carnival, Mardi Gras. The fact that the place was buzzing with noise and crowds allowed the young man – a singer destined for immortality – to enjoy, for this moment at least, a little anonymity among the merry-makers.

Elvis Presley had come to this heartland of the Blues – pronounced throughout the South as "Noo Orlins" – on this night of 4 February 1955 for a one-night stand at the Blue Star Club, one of dozens of night spots in the Vieux Carré, part of the city's old French quarter. With his

Left: **New Orleans – the Birthplace of the Blues – in 1955.**

Right: **The Blue Star Club where Elvis played as a virtual unknown in February 1955.**

guitarist Scotty Moore, and bass player Bill Black, he was to feature in a two-hour show, promoted by disc jockey Red Smith and starring comic Bud Deckleman.

Though Elvis was beginning to become something of a celebrity in the South, his appearance did not single him out especially amidst the crowds of casually dressed revellers spilling in and out of the bars, clubs and restaurants along the one hundred blocks that make up the French quarter. His long, slicked-back hair, casual jacket and jeans identified him unmistakably as a Southern boy – although on closer inspection, the long sideburns were certainly a little unusual, and the blue, dreamy eyes and full lips curled into a sneer were unquestionably unique. He also had a sexual magnetism about him that seemed to indicate maturity way beyond his twenty years.

It is perhaps understandable that the area should have attracted the boy – the musical appeal notwithstanding. For the whole city has a heavy, decadent charm about it that somehow matches Elvis' own personality. New Orleans generally has a sleepy sensuality that is really brought to life only by the music it has inspired – just as the young

Elvis in New Orleans: (*Above*) performing in the Blue Star Club; (*left*) sight-seeing; and (*overleaf*) with Scotty Moore's 1954 Chevrolet in which the group travelled.

singer himself became a man possessed when he took a guitar in his hands and let rip with that special blend of the Blues and country music that he fused into something called rock 'n' roll, which was beginning to stir the minds and emotions of the nation's youth.

Elvis had travelled the four hundred miles to New Orleans from his home town of Memphis, Tennessee in an already well-worn 1954 Chevrolet Bel Air belonging to Scotty Moore – a vehicle bought on credit by the guitarist's wife! Neither Elvis – later to become the owner of dozens of ostentatious and expensive automobiles – nor the other member of the trio, Bill Black, had a car; and all three had piled into the vehicle complete with their instruments and changes of clothes. The three were, in fact, typical of thousands of such combos touring the small towns of America playing everywhere from the backs of flatbed trucks in the open air to school gymnasiums and local theatres. Typical, that is, except for what history had in store for them.

As the show in which the trio was appearing was not due to begin until 9 a.m., Elvis had decided to leave Scotty and Bill to have a meal while he took a walk in the French quarter. In Basin Street, he stood transfixed in the birthplace of a legend, unprepossessing though it may have been. For it was amidst this cluster of buildings, once resplendent with their wrought-iron gates and balustrades, tiled roofs and enclosed patios, now rather tatty and dirty, that the Blues were born at the turn of the century. Here it was that the Negro labourers from the cotton fields and the docks once gathered to drink, talk about their problems and express their deepest emotions through song, usually accompanied only on a battered old guitar. This was something that the young Elvis could readily understand, for much that was stirring in himself went into his music.

Through the noise of the traffic in the street, and the general hubbub caused by the carnival, Elvis could hear the occasional refrain of music issuing from behind the half-open shuttered windows in the houses and through the doors along subterranean passageways. Just then, the more strident sound of a jazz band reached his ear from somewhere nearby, and he decided to find its source.

It was in Bourbon Street, once synonymous with jazz, that he came across a jazz band parading slowly by. But something else also caught his attention: a large number of half-dressed girls who were seductively importuning the men passing by. His Mama had told him all about such girls! For a moment he stood gawping at them like any other tourist, the crooked smile on his face spreading a little further over his sallow features, and then, almost reluctantly, he walked on.

After a while Elvis reached Jackson Square, the heart of the city, beyond which lies the old French market. There he spotted a coffee stand selling doughnuts, and all of a sudden he felt quite hungry. While he ate two doughnuts and drank a Coke, his mind turned to the show at the Blue Star. He glanced at his watch – it was almost a quarter after eight. Swallowing the last mouthful of his drink, he began to retrace his steps through the Vieux Carré.

Elvis had no way of knowing, as he crossed the square and ventured into the busy network of streets beyond, that his journey to stardom would bring him back to New Orleans again – although in very different circumstances. First, as a headliner to play not a tiny night club, but the Municipal Auditorium in front of 13,000 people; and then in 1958, as a film star to make *King Creole* – a movie which remained his favourite for the rest of his life.

Presley lies brutally beaten, just a heap on the ground. But bashings such as this are worth while career-wise

In his first attempt at serious acting, Presley is involved in a street fight. He's got to make a lasting impression on picturegoers—so an impression is made on him

Against the background of the New Orleans French quarter, he flees from an assailant

NOW IT'S BALLAD WITH A BEAT-UP

YOUR new-look Elvis Presley squints through a bruised and bleeding black eye. Disillusioned? It's a sight that will have to satisfy you for two years. And it's producer Hal Wallis's insurance against the bursting bubble of rock 'n roll. *King Creole* is going to be the toughest thing you've seen.

The fear—and Presley shares it—is that Presley is not on safe ground any longer, that his popularity as a singer is headed for the exit. So it's not by chance that he plays a cruel brute in a brutal film.

Presley gets into more scraps, takes more beatings and faces more violence than probably any actor in screen history. That includes even the old-time tough guys like George Raft, Humphrey Bogart, James Cagney and Edward G. Robinson.

And all the attention of the studio is centred on making Presley an actor. That's fair enough. But what sort of actor? He is in a rôle, the movie-makers claim, that could be played by Marlon Brando or the late James Dean. He's the traditional crazy-mixed-up downtrodden kid with the world against him.

Producer Hal Wallis has the reputation of a star-builder. He had Presley pegged from the start. He was quick to see the box office potential of the then up-and-coming young rock singer. He has a contract in his pocket with Presley's signature on it. One that's been pulling in the money.

And Wallis is astute enough to know that picturegoers are going to need something more in Presley's films. "King Creole" has got to stick in your mind for two years while Presley is in the U.S. Army. So the accent is on acting.

Why bother? Although Presley's films have paid off it's not because of the star's acting ability or because they were fine films. The first, *Love Me Tender*, was far from it. *Loving You* had a better cast, a more polished production. But it was Presley's singing that started the queues. His third and most recent over here, *Jailhouse Rock*, still didn't separate Presley from his personality. But now the idea of Presley being something more than just a voice on screen has been hammered home.

But could be that within the next two years the new-look Presley will be as old-fashioned and as forgotten as last year's hat. Unless you go for that black eye.

CLARENCE RAWLINGS

Elvis returns to New Orleans as a star to film *King Creole* in 1958. (*Left*) Signing autographs for fans; (*above*) one of the many magazine features on the making of the picture; and (*overleaf*) performing in the Blue Shade Club.

On neither of these occasions, though, was Elvis to have another opportunity to wander the streets of New Orleans and enjoy the sights. Travelling to and from his concert would require bodyguards and a fast car, and when producer Hal Wallis brought a film crew to the French quarter to film the story of a young night-club barman who makes good as a singer, the area was so besieged by ecstatic fans that he had to hire a special detachment of police to keep them at bay during shooting. Elvis, for his part, had several times to leave the location over the rooftops of two or three houses to reach a waiting car!

But thoughts of such acclaim were far from the mind of the singer as he made his way to the Blue Star. Indeed, the reaction to his performance that night was to be such that he would question whether he could ever return to this city – or any other, for that matter – if that was what city folk thought of him and his music. For, as he recalled while filming *King Creole*, "We only played to 75 people the first time I came to New Orleans – and there seemed to be more people on the stage than in the audience. I even had to borrow petrol money to get to my next date in Shreveport!"

10216-45

One of the most commonly held fallacies in the legend of Elvis Presley is that he rose to fame almost literally overnight. The truth is that he spent months learning to be a singer under the tutelage of Scotty and Bill, then worked a back-breaking year and more on the road perfecting his style before audiences of all sizes in one backwoods town after another, before one unique record, "Heartbreak Hotel", not only finally established his fame in America, but made him an international star, too.

A photograph of Elvis taken at Humes High School for the 1952 Yearbook; and (*above right*) Gladys and Vernon Presley with their famous son.

The details of Elvis' early life are well documented now. Born on 8 January 1935 in a two-room shack in Tupelo, Mississippi, the only surviving twin of share-cropper Vernon Presley and his wife Gladys, the young Elvis was taken in 1948 by his impoverished father to Memphis, where Vernon hoped to find work. Here the boy had an undistinguished career at Humes High School, highlighted only by his showing his potential talent for music when he sang two songs, "Old Shep" and "Cold, Cold, Icy Fingers", at the 1952 school Christmas concert organized by Mrs Mildred Scrivener. Elvis accompanied himself on a twelve-dollar guitar bought for him by his mother, who had long been impressed by his love of music and readiness to break into song, either

A slightly romanticized picture-strip version
of Elvis' early life! (*Mirabelle* magazine,

December 1960).

at their church, the First Assembly of God Church, or in the family home.

The following year, Elvis, now a truck driver, decided to repay his mother's kindness by making a record for her as a birthday present at the little Memphis Recording Studio at 706 Union Avenue – the home of Sun Records, owned by Sam Phillips. Phillips, an Alabama-born former radio engineer and disc jockey in his twenties, had set up the studio in 1952 to produce "vanity" discs and also commercially to record rhythm and blues artists.

While Elvis was cutting the two songs for his disc – "My Happiness" (a hit song by his favourite group, the Ink Spots) and "That's When Your Heartaches Begin" – he was overheard by the studio's office manager, Marion Keisker (who was also an announcer at the all-woman local radio station, WHER). Here, Marion herself takes up the story.

66 When Elvis first came into the studio I wondered if he wanted a handout! We got a lot of drifters along Union Avenue and his hair was long and shaggy and his clothes were well worn. He was impatient and ill at ease. He was carrying a guitar and said he wanted to make a record.

I asked him what he sang and he said he could sing anything – popular songs, country and western and rhythm and blues, he said he could sing them all. I told him the price of making a record was four dollars, and sent him into the studio. Because I was curious about him, I listened in when he started to sing and he was certainly *unusual*! He seemed to be mixing all the different styles together. So I made a tape of him and got about a third of 'My Happiness' and all of 'That's When Your Heartaches Begin'. You see, over the years Sam had been saying, 'If I could find a white man who had the Negro sound and the Negro feel for music, I could make a million dollars.' And that's what I thought Elvis had. **99**

Sam Phillips now takes over the threads of the next stage in the making of the Presley legend.

66 My business was to look for singing talent, no matter what polish it was in. Of course, none of us knew he was going to be *that* big:

Sam Phillips of Sun Records, the man who sensed the young Elvis' potential.

but the minute I heard the guy sing – it was an Ink Spots tune – I knew he had a unique voice. Now there are very few things that I would say are unique, but Elvis had one of them.

I called my friend Scotty Moore and I said to him, 'I've got a young man and he's different.' I told him to get to work on Elvis, and I said, 'He's really nervous and timid and polite, but he sure has talent. He knows he's got talent, too, he just needs to get some confidence.'

Well, we got Bill Black in to help as well and it took us a while. We worked off and on with Elvis for about six months. I knew there were lots of things we could've cut, but they weren't *different*. It was up to me to see the uniqueness of his talent and go, hopefully, in the right direction with it. **99**

Elvis signs a recording contract with Sam Phillips.

Though the contributions of both Sam Phillips and Bill Black are undeniable in the developing of Elvis' raw talent, most critics are now agreed that it was Scotty Moore who did most to influence what became the "Elvis Presley sound". He has rightly been called the "great unsung hero in Elvis' life". Scotty himself insists modestly, "I can't say who was chiefly responsible for Elvis' sound because we all were. It just happened. After that we knew we had something – we had a beginning to build on."

Despite the fact that he was only a boyish-looking twenty-one at the time, Winfield Scott "Scotty" Moore, from Gadston, Tennessee, was already something of a music veteran in Memphis, having been playing guitar since he was eight and appearing with a group, the Starlight Wranglers, for several years. A quiet and serious man by nature, he had also been friendly with Sam Phillips for some time and lent a hand in the studio boss's search for the elusive "unique" singer. When Sam told Scotty about Elvis, he agreed to listen to the young singer. Scotty recalls:

66   I called Elvis up one Saturday night and invited him over to
my house the following day. When he came over he was wearing this
pink shirt and pink trousers and had a DA hairstyle and I thought my
wife would go out of the door! Anyhow, we sang some country and
western songs by Hank Snow and Marty Robbins and then a few rhythm
and blues numbers. While we were playing, Bill Black, who lived a few
doors away, stopped by. He hung around for a bit and then left before
Elvis had finished.   99

Twenty-eight-year-old William "Bill" Black, also a Tennessean, was if
anything an even more experienced musician, who had been playing his
upright bass as a session man and with various groups in the South for
almost a decade. A man of unquenchable good humour, he was noted
for his stage performances when he would often throw his bass in the
air and occasionally even sit astride it while he played! He was, frankly,
not that impressed by the young man singing with Scotty. Some years
later, Bill remembered:

66   I went back to Scotty's place after Elvis had gone, and he said,
'What do you think of him?' Well, I replied that he didn't impress me
too damn much. Seemed like a snotty-nosed kid with all those wild
clothes. Still, I had to agree he had a voice.
   'Yeah,' Scotty said, 'The thing is he needs the right material, the right
songs.' So Scotty rang Sam Phillips and told him, and he asked the three
of us to go into the studio and put a few tracks down. To begin with, I
don't think any of us thought we were going places, but we got to like
each other, and once Elvis happened on that song, 'That's All Right,
Mama', we knew we had found something.   99

The day the trio "found something", to quote Bill Black, was around
5 July 1954, and actually several false starts were made before Elvis
quite by chance began to sing and play the Arthur Crudup 1940s classic
blues song, "That's All Right, Mama". Scotty and Bill quickly picked up
on the youngster's exuberant version, and in that moment white country
music and the black people's blues were fused into a raw new style
which in time became Elvis' unique brand of rock 'n' roll.

Opposite: **"A snotty-nosed kid in wild clothes" – Bill Black's first assessment of Elvis.**

It was, with hindsight, astonishing that this conjunction should have taken place in the deeply segregational South – and naturally enough it created considerable problems in an area where any white man who sang black music faced censure and even outright hostility. This applied not only to the singer, but also to the record maker who released such material. Scotty Moore expressed these feelings with more than a little prophetic insight when he commented to his two partners during the playback of their first record, "My God, when they hear that they'll run us out of town!"

This revolutionary first Elvis Presley session for Sam Phillips also generated a number of other songs which would later be released by the company, including, "I Love You Because", "Harbour Lights", and "Blue Moon of Kentucky". It was this last track that Sam Phillips decided to release as the B side of "That's All Right, Mama", thereby linking a completely revamped classic blues number with a similarly adapted standard country song.

Sam Phillips' tiny recording studio where Elvis, Scotty and Bill cut their first Sun record, "That's All Right, Mama" in July 1954.

Elvis' debut record received its first public airing over the local radio
station, WHBQ, thanks to Sam Phillips' friendship with the resident DJ,
Dewey Phillips, who despite his name was no relation. Dewey listened
to the disc with growing excitement and at the end declared, "That'll
flat git it!" Local listeners to his show shared his enthusiasm, and by the
end of the year "That's All Right, Mama" had sold just under 20,000
copies. Good enough, in fact, for Sam to call Elvis, Scotty and Bill back
to his studios in September 1954 to cut a second disc which featured
new versions of two more classics, "Good Rockin' Tonight" and "I Don't
Care if the Sun Don't Shine".

Despite the local success of these discs, Elvis carried on with his job
as a truck driver. He did, though, manage to get some work appearing
live at one or two local night spots including The Eagle's Nest in
Memphis, where he was paid the princely sum of ten dollars per show!
However, a bigger booking which Sam Phillips obtained for the trio in
the prestigious Grand Ole Opry show in Nashville, to promote their

**An early publicity photograph of Elvis, Scotty
and Bill taken in the Sun recording studio.**

**Elvis was just one of the performers on
Louisiana Hayride, as this old photograph
taken in 1954 and found in the
programme's archives reveals.**

records, proved an unhappy experience for Elvis in front of the died-in-the-wool country and western fans who packed the Ryman Auditorium. But he was more successful on the Saturday-night radio show *Louisiana Hayride*, broadcast from Shreveport, and as a result was offered a regular weekly spot which he accepted with delight. It was not, though, until almost the end of the year that Elvis felt sure enough in his own mind that he could make a living as a singer, and quit his job.

It was on 18 December, while appearing on *Louisiana Hayride*, that Elvis first enjoyed the luxury of another backing musician – pianist Floyd Cramer. Born in Shreveport in 1933, Cramer had been playing since childhood (five years old, to be exact), and had joined *Hayride* in 1951. Here, for some years he accompanied many of the leading country and western artists, before breaking away to become a solo star and making several worldwide hits including the famous "Last Date".

"I knew Elvis in Shreveport before he was at all well known," Floyd said a few years ago, talking about what was to prove the first of many dates with him. "He was polite and shy off stage, but once he started performing – man, was he something! Even then you could tell he was goin' places."

Just how soon Elvis was "goin' places" was to become evident in the new year in the hectic months which immediately followed his twentieth birthday on 8 January 1955.

Memphis disc jockey Dewey Phillips, the first man to play Elvis' record on the air.

Rare photograph of Elvis playing at The Eagle's Nest in Memphis in 1954.

in person
THE SENSATIONAL
RADIO·RECORDING
STAR

Slim
WHITMAN

with Billy Walker, Ellis Presley and many others
Tonight One Big Show—8:00 P.M.
dv. reserved seats today at Walgreen's. Main and Union,
.00. Tonight at Shell, $1.25 reserved; kids, 75c; general ad-
mission $1.00.

OVERTON PARK SHELL

Elvis on *Louisiana Hayride* with Jimmy
Rodgers Snow, son of the famous country
and western star Hank Snow.

**In another of his early appearances in
Memphis, Elvis' name was misspelled as
"Ellis", as this 1954 advertisement shows!**

The beginning of the third decade of Elvis' life held more promise for
him than any time previously. Royalties from the sales of his Sun
records were starting to materialize, and he also began to get more
bookings for live performances not only in Memphis but further afield.
He followed a "Grand Prize Saturday Night Jamboree" at the Eagle's
Hall, Houston on New Year's night, for example, with a date on 6
January at Texas Bill Strength's night club in Atlanta. Sam Phillips also
took the opportunity of his young discovery's birthday to release a third
disc, "Milkcow Blues Boogie" backed with "You're a Heartbreaker",
which he had cut with Scotty and Bill just before Christmas.

Since making their first record together – and because Elvis was still a
minor – Scotty Moore had acted as his agent, taking a modest ten per
cent from the singer's earnings. But increasingly Scotty found this duty
interfering with his playing, and so that same month he was happy to
turn the job over to a Memphis disc jockey and show manager named
Robert "Bob" Neal. Bob was a hard-working man in his middle thirties
who had a talent for promotion and specialized in organizing small
concerts throughout the region and then publicizing them on his radio
show. With five sons, the oldest two teenagers, he was kept abreast of

Floyd Cramer, Elvis' first pianist.

Bob Neal (*left*) who was Elvis' first manager, with two Memphis disc jockeys, Ira Cole (*centre*) and Dewey Phillips, listening to the young singer's third record, "Milkcow Blues Boogie".

what was happening among young people, and it was they who urged him to pick up on the emerging talent of Elvis Presley.

Elvis' first appearance under the Neal banner was at a concert in the Overton Park Shell in Memphis. It was here that the pelvic shake which was to make him so famous – and infamous – was first revealed. Elvis himself has recalled the event in these words:

66 I was on a show in Memphis when I started doing it. I was an extra added attraction – and when I came out on the stage I was scared stiff. My first big appearance in front of an audience.

I started doing 'That's All Right, Mama' and everybody was hollerin' and screaming. And when I came off stage my manager told me they were hollering because I was wiggling. Well, when I went back for an encore I did a little more. And the more I did, the wilder they went!

I don't think it really struck me until later that night. I couldn't get to sleep, and I had this feeling that for the first time in my life I was at the beginning of something big and wonderful. Those screams could mean the end of the money worries and poverty Mom and Dad had known all their lives. **99**

One of Bob Neal's early advertisements for
Elvis, promoting him as a
country and western singer!

Bob Neal himself sometimes appeared on Elvis' early shows, and his zany mixture of ukelele playing and comic stories was undoubtedly an audience puller – that is, until the impact of the sullen-looking young singer in flashy clothes very much overshadowed the veteran in the eyes of the young audiences. But then, with fifteen per cent of the action going into his pocket, why should he worry too much?

These shows were staged in small halls and schoolhouses anywhere from fifty to a hundred miles from Memphis. Initially, Elvis' limited repertoire allowed him to perform for twenty minutes, but this rapidly grew to forty minutes as the teenagers started clamouring for curtain calls. Reminiscing about these early days of their journey to fame, Scotty Moore said a while later:

66 We'd drive way out into the country to some little place you'd never heard of. We'd get there maybe an hour before time and start setting things up. Nobody would be in sight. Then all of a sudden people would begin to turn up, and once Elvis got on it was like an

avalanche. They'd be hanging from the rafters before we'd
finished! **"**

On 12 January Bob Neal sent Elvis on his first package show of one-
night stands through the South with a group of artists from *Louisiana
Hayride*, including an up-and-coming young brother and sister act from
Shreveport, J.E. and Maxine Brown. Beginning in Clarksdale,
Mississippi, the show went on to Helena in Arkansas, then through
Booneville, Mississippi, stopped at Sheffield, Alabama, and continued
in Leachville, Arkansas. From here, Elvis, Scotty and Bill had the
chance to double back quickly to Memphis for the weekend.

For Elvis it was a chance to enjoy some of his favourite home cooking.
Later he was to say, "When I'm home, that's when I really eat. On the
road, I hardly have any appetite." In his early publicity, Elvis actually
listed eating as one of his hobbies, and his favourite foods as deluxe
cheeseburgers, coconut cake and chocolate milk-shakes! He later
recalled:

**Two dramatic pictures of Elvis performing in
the open air in Memphis. Note the addition
of D.J. Fontana on drums.**

66   My mother worried constantly about me when I was on the
road away from home. She didn't approve of it really – she thought I
wasn't taking care of myself. She was there at a few of my early concerts
and saw the crowds screaming. She got very upset, but I told her it was
going to keep on happening. At least I hoped so, because it meant they
liked me and would buy my records.   99

**Elvis loved his mother's home cooking when
he had time to return to Memphis.**

Scotty Moore also remembers these days:

66   There were all kinds of experiences in the early days. Fights
sometimes, show dates cancelled, not getting paid – it was fairly rough,
and every time before we set out, Elvis' mother would call either Bill or
myself and say, 'You be sure and take care of my boy', and we'd assure
her that we would.

I suppose you could say Elvis was a typical wild kid to begin with. I
don't mean wild in a dangerous way, but he loved pranks and practical
jokes. We also had trouble getting him out of bed in the morning, too,
which was typical. But actually I guess I wasn't that much older than
him myself!   99

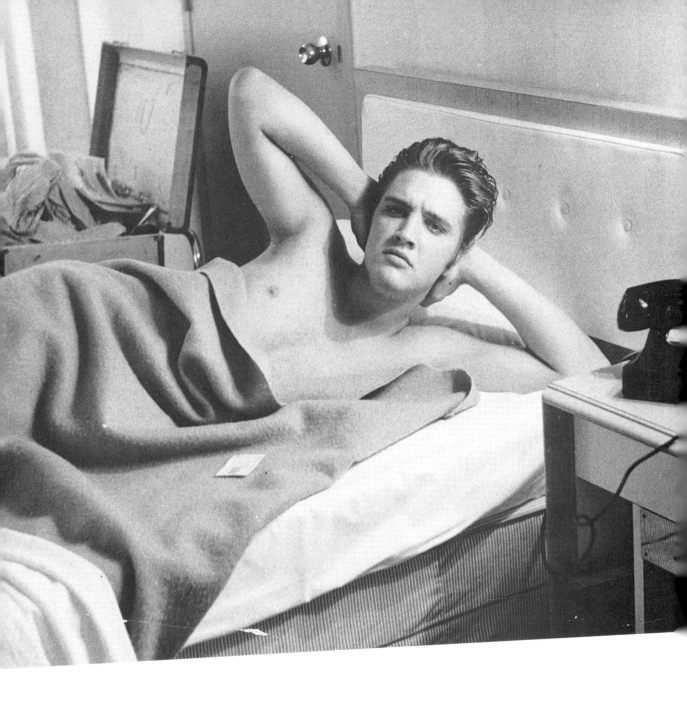

On 24 January Elvis, Scotty and Bill began a week-long sweep through east Texas with another country singer, Tom Perryman. With hindsight, it might be argued that Perryman, a local boy from Gladewater, was included in the package just in case Elvis' brand of music did not grab the paying customers. But in fact, Elvis was the one they applauded most vigorously, and with the passing months Texas was to prove to be the first place outside the vicinity of Memphis where he became really popular.

Getting out of bed in the morning was always a problem for Elvis when he was on the road – and was even mentioned on an early publicity card!

ELVIS PRESLEY

Born 8th January,
1935, in Mississippi
—has brown hair
and blue eyes. His
pet dislike is get-
ting up early in
the mornings!

After winding up this tour in the town of Midland, the trio headed
further south for New Orleans and Elvis' unforgettable visit to the home
of the Blues. And even before that night was out, the boys were back on
the road for Shreveport and their weekly date on *Louisiana Hayride*.

It was on the *Hayride* show that Elvis was first accompanied by a
drummer, D.J. Fontana, who was actually an employee of the
programme. Fontana, a darkly handsome young man with a wry sense of
humour, was another Southern boy who had been playing the drums
since childhood. He was also rather more astute than many other
musicians, preferring the safety of regular work on *Hayride* to the
uncertainty – not to mention back-breaking grind – of touring with a
group. Yet, when he was invited to join Elvis' little entourage, he didn't
hesitate. For even then (he still says today) he sensed that the boy from
Memphis with the long sideburns was something special. But Elvis was
not an instant success, as D.J. recalls.

❝   The first time he played the *Hayride* in 1954 he wasn't exactly
a sensation. He didn't get a standing ovation or anything like that. He
was moving around the stage like he always did. Those people in the
audience were used to traditional country stars – they didn't know quite

how to react. But soon the word got around about this kid and we started getting a younger crowd in. That's what did it. For he sure had something – even back then I knew it, but I couldn't put my finger on it. Now we'd call it charisma! 🙰🙰

D.J. Fontana, the drummer who joined Elvis from *Louisiana Hayride*.

D.J. says that the trio had been thinking of adding a drummer to their group for a while, and he was actually approached to join them in February 1955.

🙶🙶 Scotty and Bill asked me if I would work with Elvis. I said, 'Well, sure, but I really don't know what you're doing. I'll have to listen to you.' So we went back to the dressing room, all of us, and ran over 'That's All Right, Mama', and a couple of things like that. Elvis was a lot different from the basic country artists I'd worked with – he was between what you'd call rockabilly, hillbilly, rhythm and blues and gospel. He was a mixture of everything put together. **99**

When D.J. began touring with Elvis he soon found it was every bit as hard as he had expected – but never uneventful.

Elvis would drink bottles of Coca Cola after a performance.

66 I first went out on the road with them for shows in Texas. Driving on those wide old roads, we'd stop – it seemed – like every few miles. We always had trouble making time. There were all these roadside stands and Elvis would want to stop at every one to buy Cokes. He had a lot of nervous energy and he just couldn't stay still for very long. **99**

Elvis himself later talked about his inability to control this streak of mischievousness.

66 Bill, Scotty and D.J. would get real upset with me because I wanted to stop at every roadside stand and load up the car. Sometimes I would stay at the stands a little longer than I should and then be late for the next show. There were times they threatened to take me to the nearest airport to catch a plane to the next show – but I never took that real serious because we didn't have the money to fly! We could go on and on without even thinking about a real night's sleep. Drive and perform, drive and perform, and drive some more. It was wild, man, but it was fun! **99**

One rather wild trick the three older members of the group all remember Elvis playing during these journeys was to buy firecrackers, light them, and then throw them out of the window of the speeding car at the billboards along the side of the road!

D.J. says that a lot of the early shows the group played were at the most unlikely places – including in front of grain stores! More often than not, they played on the backs of trucks. "You could really see the reactions on people's faces, they were so close to us," he smiles at the memory. "Then we moved up to the big time – playing high-school gyms!"

During his lifetime, Elvis more than once reminded interviewers that his fame did not come easily or quickly – though few of them chose to record this – and D.J. Fontana recalls a vivid example of this fact.

> ❝ It happened at a place called Lakecliff when we played this night club in a kind of shack-up motel. For years they had been used to having a country band on Friday and Saturday nights, and it usually got so busy you couldn't stir the place with a stick. Well, I guess they were expecting their regular band until we came on. They just stared at us.
>
> Anyhow, Elvis started singing and jumping and we were hollering in back of him. You never saw a place empty so sharply. 'That's not Hoot and Curly!' they said, and left. By the time we finished there weren't more than a handful of folks left. They just weren't ready for Elvis.
>
> They never booked us again. They said we ruined the place – wouldn't even let us stay in the motel! ❞

Elvis on the road – four photographs taken by a fan in Memphis in 1956.

Elvis was happy to admit to this and other similar examples of setbacks in his early days on the road. In an interview in the mid 'sixties, he said:

> ❝ I wasn't exactly an overnight success. It was a lot of hard work. Travelling, sleepless nights – a couple of years at least. I remember some of the little towns we went to; sometimes they'd be having a country

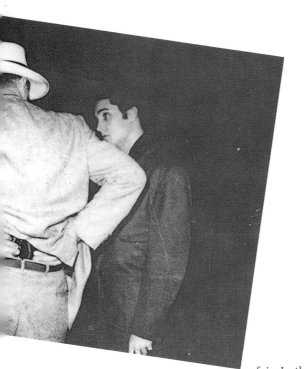

fair. In the middle of the place would be a stage set up on a platform or a truck. We'd go on after the local talent and play my records. Often the men and women, even the babies and dogs, would go on with their business as if we weren't there. Talking and arguing and laughing and making such a din we couldn't be heard. Sometimes, though, there would be a few girls at the front freaking out and I knew at least I was getting through to someone. **99**

Life for Elvis and the other three could be just as hard in-between shows. He remembered:

66   We spent a lot of time on the road in those early days, but we never had enough money for things. We pooled our money for hamburgers and many times we slept in the car because we didn't have the money for a hotel. Sometimes we'd drive all night to get to where we were performing, and as soon as we'd finished drive all night again to the next show.

   We had a lot of problems with transportation. The automobiles would break down, and then we'd have to put what little money we did earn into a new car so we could get to the next job. There were even times when the cars would break down and we'd have to hitch-hike or wire for the money for a bus! It was very hard work and there were times I thought I should quit and go back to being a truck driver like my Daddy said. But I loved the crowds, the people, the applause. **99**

Downcast as Elvis obviously got from time to time, his will to succeed and his belief in his music kept him going. There were, happily, occasional highlights to revive his faith – such as his guest appearance on a jamboree show in Memphis at the Ellis Auditorium on Sunday 6 February, which produced one of the first newspaper clippings for his scrapbook from the *Memphis Press-Scimitar*:

HILLBILLY JAMBOREE BRINGS HEADLINERS

66   A hit parade of country music is in store for patrons of the Five-Star Jamboree at 3 and 8 p.m. today in the North Hall of the Auditorium, sponsor Bob Neal promises.

Three of the five top stars on the bill are currently among the leaders in the hillbilly hit parade listings. Faron Young, who heads the cast, is rated No. 3 by disc jockeys from coast to coast in the *Billboard* magazine, while Elvis Presley, young Memphis star making a swift and spectacular rise, is rated as his home city's third best seller this past week.

Then there's Ferlin Huskey with two recordings holding down spots in the magic top ten. Not far behind are the Wilburn Brothers and Martha Carson. 99

A smartly-dressed Elvis performing in 1955.

Ferlin Husky, now a veteran of the American country and western scene, did not see Elvis' performance at this jamboree, although he was vaguely aware of some of the screaming that went on when the young singer appeared. He does, however, ruefully recall a later show in which he appeared with Elvis. In his unmistakable slow drawl, Ferlin says:

66   It was out in Texas, and as I was the headliner I asked the promoter, Bob Neal, if I could close the show after Elvis. Bob said sure, he didn't think it would make any difference to Elvis. So I went on after Elvis and all I heard was the kids calling for him to come back! I had to go to Bob after I came off and say, 'I think we had better go back to the way you had the show set up the first time!' Elvis was some act – you just didn't follow him unless you were crazy. 99

SUNDAY - FEB. 6

TWO SHOWS ★ 3:00 p.m. & 8:00 p.m.

AUDITORIUM

MEMPHIS, TENN.

FARON YOUNG

★ "IF YOU AIN'T LOVIN"

MARTHA CARSON

★ BEAUTIFUL GOSPEL SINGER

FERLIN HUSKEY

THE HUSHPUPPIES

Doyle and Teddy

WILBURN BROTHERS

Plus... MEMPHIS' OWN

ELVIS PRESLEY

SCOTTY and BILL

He'll Sing "HEARTBEAKER" - "MILK COW BOOGIE"

MANY MORE...

After his appearance in Memphis, Elvis and his group hit the road again, playing shows in Ripley, Mississippi and Alpine, Texas. The end of the week saw them travelling into New Mexico for a show and dance appearance with singer Lee Hamric in the town of Carlsbad. This is situated near to the spectacular Sacramento Mountains on the River Pecos, and it was perhaps a portent of things to come that Elvis got there thanks to the man who was later to help him scale the highest peaks of success – Colonel Tom Parker.

Though Elvis was probably unaware of the fact at the time, the two shows in Carlsbad had been set up in a deal Bob Neal had made with the Colonel's Jamboree Attractions company based in Madison, Tennessee. Colonel Parker had yet actually to see the young man in action, but with his ear constantly to the ground for new talent, news of Elvis and his special brand of music had already reached him. For the moment, though, the Colonel was content to watch and wait and see how far Bob Neal could take the boy.

By now Elvis had, in fact, notched up some impressive statistics which were pointers to what lay ahead. In the past three months he had played getting on for fifty dates, travelled some 25,000 miles, and the total sales for his three Sun releases were – according to another article in the *Memphis Press-Scimitar* – "over 300,000 and still going". The paper also reported that Bob Neal had just put Elvis on a more businesslike footing by opening up offices at 160 Union Avenue, Memphis, under the bold sign, "Elvis Presley Enterprises".

In this article, rather curiously headlined "Suddenly Singing Elvis Presley Zooms into Recording Stardom", a newspaper staff writer, Robert Johnson, described what he called "momentous changes for a young man who likes to sing and play the guitar" and quoted a local record-shop owner, Ruben Cherry, as saying, "Just three records and every one has been a hit. People have come in to buy them who never bought a record before."

Of Elvis himself Johnson reported: "He now has enough money to buy all the cheeseburgers he wants. When he has music on his mind, he forgets eating, then gets a terrific appetite which may demand eight cheeseburgers and three milk-shakes at a sitting!" According to the same journalist, Elvis was also getting fan letters addressed to the office on

"The Hillbilly Cat" in action – photograph taken in 1955.

Opposite: Rare poster for Elvis' appearance in Memphis in February 1955.

Union Avenue, requesting autographs and photographs.

Robert Johnson was quick to pay tribute to Sam Phillips for his part in the singer's rise, claiming that the boss of Sun records was "largely responsible for a new trend in the field which the trade publications call R & B (for rhythm and blues) and country (or hillbilly) music . . . Sam doesn't know how to categorize Elvis exactly for he has a white voice, sings with a negro rhythm which borrows in mood and emphasis from country style."

As a result of this conglomeration of different types of music, the ever-enthusiastic Marion Keisker told Johnson she had nicknamed the young singer "The Hillbilly Cat" – a phrase derived from the Texas term for rhythm and blues: "cat music".

The newspaperman concluded his report:

66 While he appears with so-called hillbilly shows, Elvis' clothes are strictly sharp. His eyes are darkly slumbrous, his hair sleekly long, his sideburns low, and there is a lazy, sexy, tough, good-looking manner which bobby soxers like. Not all record stars go over as well on stage as they do on records. Elvis sells.

If the merry-go-round doesn't start spinning too fast for a 20-year-old, he'll end up with enough cheeseburgers to last a Blue Moon. Spin 'em again, boys! 99

"He has a lazy, sexy, tough, good-looking manner which bobby soxers like" – *Memphis Press-Scimitar*, **February 1955.**

This article was undoubtedly of tremendous publicity value to Elvis – all the more so when it was syndicated to other newspapers in the "musical triangle" where he was appearing: south-west Arkansas, northern Louisiana and east Texas. The reference to his sex appeal, while certainly adding to the momentum among the young, also began to stir the first flames of opposition which were to be generated around his stage act as winter turned into a warm spring and then a summer that was to prove red hot in more ways than one.

2 the hottest singer in the west

Another clear sign that Elvis was on his way towards a crock of gold also came in February 1955, when a disc jockey named Mike Michael of KDMS in the appropriately named town of El Dorado, Arkansas began putting his not inconsiderable clout behind promoting Elvis every week over the air waves of the South. Like Dewey Phillips in Memphis, Mike was a man who could spot new talent and sense new trends, attributes which had given him a large following among young people. He had been playing Elvis' records since the release of "That's All Right, Mama" the previous year, but it was the increasing demands he received from his listeners for *both* sides of Elvis' third record, "Milkcow Blues Boogie" backed with "You're a Heartbreaker", that prompted him to start running a special fifteen-minute segment of his show three times a week solely devoted to the young singer from Memphis.

The enthusiastic response to these spots caused Mike to contact Bob Neal and arrange a live jamboree performance in the El Dorado high-school auditorium on 14 February. A full house of ecstatic fans left Mike in no doubt that his gamble had been well worth the trouble. He later recalled:

Giving it all he's got — an outstanding photograph by Bob Moreland of Elvis in performance.

" From the moment Elvis appeared with Scotty and Bill it was pandemonium. I'd never seen a performance like it. He just did things on stage that whipped 'em all up!

He came on with that crooked, boyish grin of his. Then he threw back a long hank of brown hair from his eyes, let his guitar hang loose and leant into the microphone. He swayed his body a mite, smacked his thigh, and with this great raw cry broke into 'Good Rockin' Tonight'. As he sang, he sort of jerked his shoulder, shook his left leg and rolled back on his heels – the whole place just went crazy! "

Mike particularly remembers the way Elvis would gently caress the

microphone up and down as he sang, and also how he leant forward
provocatively towards the breathless young girls in the front row of the
auditorium, his sensual blue eyes challenging, even inviting. He had
never seen such an instinctive performer, he says, and though the young
Elvis was unmistakably nervous – even from the side of the stage the
sweat could be seen standing out on his forehead before he began to sing
– the sureness of his deep Southern voice was plainly evident even
through the inefficient sound system he had to make do with.

Elvis played many Texas school auditoriums like these in 1955.

Mike Michael has often wondered since whether it was the poor quality of the microphones that Elvis used during his early days on the road which contributed to the heavily accented mumble he used when announcing what number he was going to do next. Not that after a time anyone could hear what he was saying above all the screaming! But despite the difficulties, says the Arkansas DJ, Elvis remained unfailingly polite and willing to do whatever was asked of him by those running the shows in which he appeared.

Another disc jockey who had also taken note of the impact Elvis was having in the southern states was Bill Randle of Radio Station WERE in Cleveland, Ohio, who in time was to be credited with being the first DJ in the north of America to give Elvis serious airplay. Bill was impressed enough to arrange with Bob Neal for the young singer to appear on his show – and on 19 February Elvis made his very first appearance north of the Mason-Dixon line on the *Circle Theater Jamboree*. Also appearing with him in his live broadcast show was another singer destined for international stardom, the clean-cut balladeer Pat Boone.

Interestingly, too, this show was being filmed by Universal Pictures as part of a movie they were making with the working title *A Day in the Life of a Number One DJ*, in which the phenomenal popularity that disc

jockeys were then enjoying with the American public was to be
scrutinized through the life of one of their number, Bill Randle, and the
kind of music he played. Hence, Elvis suddenly found himself part of
this filming, which covered the rehearsals, the *Jamboree* itself, and even
some backstage conversations between the DJ and a number of the
performers.

Pat Boone's ballad style of singing was very different from Elvis', and
for this reason the two were later presented by the media as great rivals.
In fact they were good friends, though their first meeting in Cleveland
did little to suggest they had much in common, as Pat himself later
recalled.

66 I had flown to Cleveland to appear in the movie and first met
Elvis backstage at the auditorium where it was being filmed. It was a
sock-hop affair and I was waiting to close the show when in walks this
guy with his coat a little too big and his pants a little too long – real
slinky, you know? I knew that it must be Elvis.

So I went over to him and put out my hand and said, 'Hi, Elvis – I'm
Pat Boone.' He said, 'Murrbbllee . . . Murrbbllee . . .' – he just mumbled
something I couldn't understand. So I said, 'Boy, Bill Randle tells me he
thinks you're really going to be big.' And again he said something like,
'Mmm . . . murrbbllee', a sort of country twang mumble. I just couldn't
tell *what* he was saying!

"When Elvis sang the whole place just went crazy" – the famous pelvic shake in action!

Now it's

BOONE

versus

PRESLEY

says Sarah Stoddart

Pat Boone's new film is about military school students who go chasing after the thrills

FOR a year they've both been swearing it's the fight that never was. But now the shadow boxing is over. It's Boone versus Presley. The two giants of the pop world have let battle commence —whether they wanted it or not. And Hollywood is promoting the contest.

Paramount rushed Presley into *King Creole* before he started his army service. Now Fox is smartly off the mark in starring Boone in *Mardi Gras*.

Any similarity is purely intentional. **Both films are set in New Orleans with titles that pair up like peas in a pod. Both are pegged as musical dramas, both studios say both singing idols get their biggest acting challenge.**

King Creole is about a high school kid tempted into crime. *Mardi Gras* is about military school students chasing thrills.

Says Presley of Boone: "I rate Pat Boone the best around today." Says Boone of Presley: "I

sometimes envy him—he can afford to be eccentric. I've become the stereotyped image of a guy who never makes a mistake."

Discland is also making a fight of it. R.C.A. is eager to show that the Presley label isn't ready for the wax museum. It is putting out "The Elvis Golden Album"—a collection of Presley discs that have each sold over a million copies. And Private Presley's progress is punctuated by recording sessions which R.C.A. arranges during his army leaves.

Meantime, the London label has countered with three LPs issued recently and now has the single "Sugar Moon" and "Chérie, I Love You."

These two top names in pop have an equal fan following. But picturegoers still have to make up their minds which dreamboat rings their box office bell. Hollywood is making certain your choice will be a tough one.

Elvis Presley counters with *King Creole*, story of a high school kid tempted into crime

---

He also had his shirt collar turned up and always seemed to be looking down, like he couldn't look up. I thought to myself, 'What's wrong with this guy?' Anyhow, I waited around and out walked Elvis on to the stage with his guitar and there were some murmurs from the audience and a few 'ooohs', because Bill had given him such an introduction. He did look interesting, though, but not like a star.

Anyhow, I watched him and the audience's reaction, and he didn't say anything. He just went into some rockabilly type song. He looked like he was laughing at something all the time – like he had some private joke, you know? The audience started to kind of get with it – they seemed to like what they heard and though they couldn't understand most of the words, the song had a kind of raw energy to it, an excitement that really got to them. He twitched and shook a little bit and then finished the song, and there was a really good hand.

Then he said, 'Thankyuvirmush . . . Murrbbllee' – that same hillbilly mumble again – and you could see the girls' faces fall a bit and almost hear them thinking, 'Oh no, he's really a hillbilly rube.' But he goes into another song and they'd forget that and the excitement would build up again. So he was fine when he was singing, but when he'd talk he'd ruin it.

Pat Boone and Elvis were described by the press as great rivals when they were, in fact, friends.

51

So he didn't, in fact, talk very much, just sang, and when he had finished there was a big hand and you could tell that he really did have this certain kind of excitement. I just said, 'Well, I guess Bill's right about this guy' – and, of course, he was. In the next few months he became the biggest thing that ever happened to the record business! **99**

Elvis' popularity in Cleveland also grew rapidly following this appearance, and his records were soon featuring high in the local charts. Such, indeed, was his impact both on the audience and the film makers that, according to popular legend, Universal decided to make Elvis the star of the movie they were shooting and rename it *The Pied Piper of Cleveland*.

That, however, is only a rumour – the fact is that the film was never released and still languishes to this day in the vaults of Universal Pictures in Hollywood. According to the company, the finished picture was considered unsuitable for release. But another version of the story insists that by the time it was ready for public showing, Colonel Tom Parker had become Elvis' manager and squashed any such plans, believing that the movie did not feature Elvis in the best light. Whichever may be the truth, Elvis' one appearance on film before he became famous has certainly never been publicly seen.

Immediately after the Cleveland date, Elvis returned to his native South once more for another jamboree concert at the town of Hope near the giant Millwood Reservoir in Arkansas. Along with Scotty and Bill, Elvis drove to the date via two prophetically named towns: Stuttgart and England. The original of the former – which was named by its early German settlers – Elvis was to see during his army stint in Europe; while the namesake of the latter, which had also been named by settlers and in time would become the home of some of his most devoted fans, was to prove one place to which he would never come closer than the English Channel, which he steamed up on his way to Germany.

Also featuring with Elvis in Hope was a varied selection of acts including the Duke of Paducah, a hillbilly comedian whose real name was Whitey Ford; Jimmy Rodgers Snow, son of the famous country and western singer Hank Snow; and Mother Maybelle Carter, a popular

"The Pied Piper of Cleveland" – Elvis looked much like this when he was filmed in 1955, although the pictures here and overleaf are actually scenes from his second movie, *Loving You*.

country singer who appeared with her daughters, Anita, Helen and June, known as the Carter Sisters. The Carters were, in fact, all members of Colonel Tom Parker's stable of acts.

June Carter, who today is married to another of the young rockabilly singers who first came to public attention recording for Sun Records in the 'fifties, Johnny Cash, remembers the young Elvis well.

❝ It was Colonel Tom Parker who brought us together, I guess you could say. I had heard about Elvis before, but the first time we appeared together was at this jamboree the Colonel presented in Hope. I was with the family, and I did my usual little comedy bit at the beginning and then we all did our set. After that Elvis and Scotty and Bill came on.

I loved the kind of music Elvis was doing – to me he was just one of a whole rockabilly group that came out of Memphis: Johnny Cash, Carl Perkins, Jerry Lee Lewis – but he made it bigger than the others. In fact, it was Elvis who introduced me to Johnny Cash, because when we went on tour, every little cafe we went into he used to put on Johnny's records. Elvis was such a big fan of his. Then one day Elvis actually introduced us at the Grand Ole Opry.

I still remember how Elvis used to tune his guitar listening to Johnny's record, 'Cry, Cry, Cry'. But he was always breaking the strings because of the way he played. Many a time I sat backstage stringing up that guitar and keeping it in tune for him. He was very appreciative, but he never took any more care not to break the strings!

The last date I played with Elvis was in his birthplace, Tupelo. You could tell he was going to be a big star. I think if only people had let him have some kind of a normal life when he wasn't performing he might still have been around today to chew over those days with Johnny and me and the other guys. **❞**

Though Elvis clearly liked June Carter, it was her older sister, the slim, brunette Anita, that really caught his eye. After their first meeting at Hope he could not get her out of his mind, and when they met again a couple of months later, Elvis was to suffer his first real bout of "puppy love".

Bill Black skilfully laying down the beat for Elvis on his double bass.

On 1 March Elvis made his television debut when NBC screened part of *Louisiana Hayride* on which he, Scotty and Bill were now increasingly popular weekly fixtures. Unfortunately, Elvis' appearance was confined to a single country song and went completely unnoticed by viewers and critics alike.

Bob Neal, however, sensed that a successful television appearance could provide a tremendous boost to Elvis' career, and arranged for him to audition for the Arthur Godfrey TV show *Talent Scouts*, which was made in New York. Together with Scotty and Bill, Elvis nervously took his first plane flight to the Big Apple in an attempt to earn an appearance on what was then the most popular and prestigious showcase for new talent.

Whether the journey unnerved Elvis (for he was to hate flying for many years – and not altogether without reason, as you will read in due course), or whether he was just too outrageous for Arthur Godfrey, it is difficult to say. But the show turned him down. Elvis made light of any disappointment he may have felt by an offhand remark to his mother when he returned to Memphis that he personally didn't think very much of New York! Bob Neal was more obviously upset by the rejection, but cheered himself up by noting the obvious impact his young client was having in live performance. Speaking years later, Neal said proudly:

66 He became a sensation every place he went in those days. First, playing around Memphis. Then, as a member of the *Louisiana Hayride*, we played a lot of concert tours across Texas. Everywhere he went, even though he wasn't known nationally, he was a tremendous hit and a great favourite.

We travelled quite a bit. He was also very ambitious at that time, and said that he really wanted to be a big singing star and a big movie star. But he was always very polite and pleasant and I enjoyed working with him very much. **99**

Someone who was an even closer eye-witness to the emergence of the young singer during these crucial months was Bill Black, skilfully laying down the beat on his bass and occasionally letting his own sense of fun and exuberance add to the pandemonium that the young Elvis was generating. In a rare and never reprinted interview given in the early 'sixties after he had begun touring with his own group, the Bill Black Combo, the versatile musician who tragically died in 1968 had this to say about his days with Elvis.

"He actually grew those sideburns to make himself look older" – Bill Black.

66 In the beginning, Elvis had curly hair and looked about twelve years old, even with his sideboards which he actually grew to make himself look older! We weren't really a group, just Elvis, Scotty and me – and, of course, D.J., who joined us later. We did have a contract, though, but we were far from rich. We formed a syndicate, splitting our money three ways with Elvis getting double what Scotty and I got. Sometimes we spent more money on fuel than food!

But we all got on swell together. We used to play penny-ante cards, read each other's crime books, visit disc jockeys wherever we stopped, taking copies of our record, and going to the movies or watching TV in our hotel rooms.

Elvis was the youngest of the four of us, but he was the boss. He was fun to be around. We used to kid him about the first time a female shouted, 'Elvis – I love you! I love you!' No, it wasn't a teenager. It was a woman who told us later she was over seventy! That was because he

was young looking, I guess. She was feeling very maternal towards
him! **99**

But as Elvis' fame grew, said Bill, so the problems increased for both the
singer and his musicians.

66 After a while it started getting dangerous working with him
because of the fans. And expensive! I had my bass stamped to splinters
in one place and my clothes plucked off like chickens eat corn. Mostly
the noise of the audience was so loud we couldn't even hear ourselves
when we hit a sour note!

But Scotty, D.J. and I got cunning later on when it came to avoiding
the fans. We used to go the opposite way Elvis went when leaving the
theatre and then make out we were part of the crowd looking for Elvis.
Much safer! **99**

This momentum in Elvis' career encouraged
Sam Phillips to call him into the Sun studio in
Memphis once again, and in April he made his
fourth disc, "Baby, Let's Play House", an old
rhythm and blues number by Arthur Gunter,
which the young rocker transformed by the
introduction of a hiccuping style of delivery
which accentuated the proposition implicit in
the title. Backed with a new country song, "I'm
Left, You're Right, She's Gone", this now
famous record was, surprisingly, to take almost
two months to reach the charts.

Interestingly, too, during March while Elvis
had appeared again at the Eagle's Hall in
Houston, five of his songs had been secretly
taped by a recording engineer who obviously
admired his style. These songs were later issued
to fans on an unofficial or "bootleg" record, and
did not surface on an acknowledged label for
public sale for over twenty years until Virgin

**"Elvis was fun to be around" – a page from
an early magazine feature on the new
Memphis singing sensation.**

"Let's take a break - I'm tired!"

"How's business?" - Elvis chats
with cashier at Loew's State,
where he once ushered.

Records in the UK finally released them in 1979!

That same April, in which Elvis' fourth record came out, also saw the launching of the first of what was later to become a worldwide network of fan clubs. The pioneer "Elvis Presley Fan Club" was started by a teenager from Dallas, Texas named Kay Wheeler, who had first seen Elvis perform earlier in the year during one of his whirlwind visits to the Lone Star State. She had been instantly captivated by his personality, energy and unique style. Talking about the reasons for founding the club, Kay told Texas newspaper reporter Bob Masters, "I flip every time I meet Elvis – he is the most fascinating human I've ever known. Elvis is a living denial of the notion teenagers should be seen and not heard."

That statement of Kay's has proved more farsighted than she may have realized, for in time, when Elvis had become famous, it would be echoed throughout America and the rest of the world. She had sensed in her young hero a determination to sing and perform his music the way he felt it should be sung regardless of what adults might say – the first salvo in the battle that young people mid-way between childhood and adulthood were to wage in order to express their own individuality. Along with film stars James Dean and Marlon Brando, Elvis was to offer the young a model of rebellion mixed with self-expression which would establish the notion of what is today known so familiarly as a "teenager".

Elvis with Kay Wheeler, who started his first fan club in Dallas; and (*right*) a membership card for his home-town fan club, the Elvis Presley Tankers.

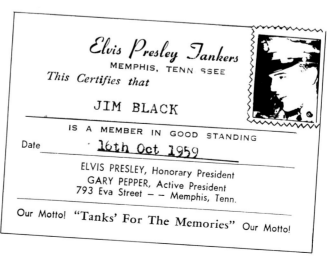

ELVIS

A now-fading photograph of Elvis and Kay Wheeler taken in 1955 remains to commemorate this new development in his career. Unhappily, however, no photograph exists of Elvis' first encounter with the man who was irrevocably to change his life, Colonel Tom Parker. This occurred the following month when Elvis set out on what Bob Neal described as the young singer's "first big tour"

Hank Snow's All-Star Jamboree was a package of talent, headlined by that veteran country and western singer, which Colonel Parker had put together for a three-week tour and which started out on 1 May from Louisiana. Continuing into Arkansas and Alabama, the show next moved on to Florida, Georgia, North Carolina and finished at Chattanooga in Tennessee. Also appearing in the jamboree were several other leading country singers including Faron Young, Slim Whitman, Jimmy Rodgers Snow, and once again Mother Maybelle Carter and the Carter Sisters.

Working once more in proximity to the lovely young Anita Carter immediately renewed Elvis' passion for the pretty singer which had

Two pictures of Elvis with Colonel Tom Parker, the man who made him a superstar; photographs of the two men together are rare.

ELVIS PRESLEY MAY FILM MANAGER'S LIFE STORY!

MGM wants Elvis Presley to star in a film based on the colourful life of his manager, Colonel Tom Parker. The project is being discussed in Hollywood with the studio, which recently signed Elvis for four films.

Called "Right This Way Folks," the story would be a dramatic one tracing the colonel's career since he was a fairground barker in Tampa, Florida.

Parker is this week doing research for "Right This Way Folks" at the Florida State Fair.

A similar event—at Seattle—will be the scene of another Presley film which goes into production this year, "Take Me To The Fair." Ted

"Cumbo Ya-Ya." This is one of a number of projects for which he is under a long-term contract to Hal Wallis.

"Cumbo Ya Ya," a Creole expression meaning "Everybody talks at once," will have Elvis playing the

An artist's impression of the moment history was made; and (*above*) one of the most unlikely of all the stories written about Elvis — that he was to play the Colonel in a film of his life story!

begun in Hope earlier in the year. Indeed, by the time the party had reached Jacksonville in Florida, all the signs were that Elvis had fallen in love.

According to a member of the Hank Snow troupe, after one particularly exhausting performance Elvis pretended to faint and allowed himself to be rushed to hospital in the hope of winning Anita's sympathy. When the young girl remained unmoved, Elvis returned to the show the following day acting as if nothing had happened.

This blow to his pride soon put a stop to Elvis' infatuation, and shortly afterwards he began paying his attentions to another female member of the party. He was obviously determined not to be discouraged by the failure of his first attempt at romance with a co-star. In fact, there were to be many more in the years that followed, both with singers and actresses – not forgetting the countless pretty young fans who also threw themselves at him in every town he visited.

However, something far more significant occurred when the promoter of the tour, Colonel Parker, decided to take a look at the latest addition to the company while the show was playing the town of Texarkana in Arkansas. A friend of the Colonel's, Paul Lichter, describes the meeting of the two men who were to change the face of pop music.

66 It was just before a matinee that the Colonel slipped into a seat to catch the act that he'd been told was driving the audience mad. He watched this young stud carry the crowd with him as he worked himself to the point of exhaustion. The Colonel glanced around him to see the people pounding the seats and floors with rhythmic approval, causing the rafters to ring with their screams. At that moment, all the years of experience gained from the thousands of days and nights with the sideshows, the carnivals, the circus, and the one-night stands hit him with a mad rush. Tom Parker could see that whatever Elvis had, it was real and vital – it was a solid talent. It was a kind of magic that comes along once in a lifetime. The poor boy from Tupelo and the old carny met backstage and the greatest union in show-business history was formed. 99

Although the association between Elvis and his manager is now a very familiar part of the Presley legend, there is a common fallacy about Parker that time has done little to erase. For though the "good ole Colonel" – as he is widely known – is generally believed to be as American as apple pie, he was actually born in Holland and the publicity tales he wove around himself are almost the equal of the success story he achieved for Elvis.

According to most reference books, Thomas Andrew Parker was born in West Virginia, on 26 June 1910, the son of parents travelling with a carnival show. The story goes that both his parents died before young Tom was ten, and he was raised by an uncle who ran "The Great Parker Pony Circus". By the time he was seventeen, the youngster had started his own show with a pony and a monkey, and he is also credited with having invented the foot-long hot-dog later sold at many an American carnival.

Sometime in the late 1940s he switched his attentions to the world of music, and became press agent for several country singers including Gene Austin and Eddy Arnold. From there it was only a short step to becoming an agent, and with this in mind he set up offices in Madison, Tennessee. The seal on his success seemed to have been achieved when he added top star Hank Snow to his roster – and so it may well have proved had he not set eyes on Elvis that fateful day. As it was, he had now found the young man on whose behalf he could concentrate all his formidable skills as a hard-nosed negotiator and determined gambler to achieve what must have seemed like unimaginable success.

Such is the legend. The facts are rather different. The Colonel was actually born on 26 June 1909 in the town of Breda, in Holland, where he was christened Andreas van Kuijk. In 1929 he left home and spent a brief period in England before moving to the West Indies. From there, a year later, he moved on to America, the famed "land of opportunity". Here he did indeed work with a travelling circus before serving in the US Army from 1931 to 1936, leaving with an injured back and a small pension. After an unsuccessful attempt to sell a "cure-everything medicine", he became a publicist and promoter, achieving such success for the Governor of the state of Louisiana, Jimmy Davis, that in 1948 he awarded him the honorary nomenclature of "Colonel" – a title which he flaunted outrageously for the rest of his life!

Curiously, Tom Parker made little mention of another publicity triumph achieved before he moved into the world of country singers. In 1947 he accompanied the famous cowboy film star Tom Mix to London, and there made front-page news by getting Mix to ride into the foyer of the Savoy Hotel, where he was staying, on the back of his horse!

As a life-long practitioner of hokum, it is perhaps not surprising that the Colonel would wish to surround his own life in mystery. He rarely gave interviews during his years of association with Elvis, although he

did once tell an American reporter, "The first thing you learn about
advertising and publicity is never to tell the truth." His credo, he said,
was "Don't explain it, sell it."

Nevertheless, Colonel Parker was, just once, a little forthcoming about
the boy he made "The King". "I think Presley was a star from the day he
ever started going into show business," he said. "I think anyone could
have helped him that knows something about show business."

Although this view may well be Colonel Tom Parker deliberately
underselling himself and what he achieved for Elvis, there are those
who think that the former sideshow hustler did not fully develop his
artist's unique talents as fully as he might have done. But of his own
value to Elvis he also had this to say:

66 I think it was my experience, and, in a small way, handling his
future by making contracts where perhaps someone would offer a
certain amount of money and I thought he was worth more and so I held
out for my price. I've lost some deals, but gained some others by
waiting . . . Elvis, when I found him, had a million dollars' worth of
talent. Now he has a million dollars. 99

Whatever Colonel Parker may have believed the future held for Elvis, he
was not yet the boy's manager in the spring of 1955 – and though he
would not become so for a few months more, the die was already cast:
the shadow of the Colonel would never be far away whenever or
wherever Elvis performed. Bob Neal, too, was also realizing that the
wheeler-dealer from Madison – whatever his background might be – had
far more to offer Elvis in terms of his career than he could ever hope to
match.

It was also true to say that when Elvis set out on this tour with Hank
Snow's All-Star Jamboree he was very much one of the supporting acts.
But as Paul Lichter's account indicates, and another report now
confirms, before the show had got very far on the road the young singer
was rapidly becoming the major attraction.

Newspaper accounts of Elvis "in concert" in the early months of 1955
are, not surprisingly, few and far between, but one writer, Ken Jones,
who later became a member of the staff of the *Memphis Press-Scimitar*,

was among the audience who saw the All-Stars in Mobile, Alabama on
6 May and has provided the following revealing pen picture of the
young rocker upstaging the forty-year-old country and western veteran
who had begun singing as a teenager in his native Canada and had
achieved lasting fame in Nashville at the Grand Ole Opry. I am grateful
to the *Press-Scimitar* for their permission to reprint this unique piece of
Presley lore.

**Elvis with country and western veteran Hank
Snow.**

66   The first act after the intermission was supposed to be a warm-
up for Hank Snow, the headliner for the country music caravan. As the
crowd drifted back from the concession stands and settled into the seats
of Ladd Stadium in Mobile, no one was in the mood for another warm-
up act.

'Let ole Hank pick and sing so we all can go home', yelled one good
ole boy as he cracked open a peanut and wiped the sweat, prompted by
a humid Gulf Coast night, from his brow. As he was yelling, some of the
crowd started chuckling.

Three guys dressed in blushing pink were taking the stage, led by a slender, but muscular young man with shaggy sideburns and slicked down ducktails. They looked out of place. Country music fans had become accustomed to stage dress of rhinestones, sequins and embroidered wagonwheels, but pink was out of character in 1955.

The chuckles were quickly drowned out. Scotty Moore unleashed his electric guitar into a pulsating frenzy. Bill Black's upright bass fell straight into a very un-country beat, and the young singer, gyrating like a congo dancer, virtually attacked the microphone. 'Have you heard the news?' he shouted, 'There's good rocking tonight!'

Mobilians were having their first encounter with Elvis Presley, and they were immediately in a state of silent shock, which lasted until the first guitar break. Then a tumultuous roar almost eclipsed the frenzied music, a roar that was to be a byproduct of Elvis Presley concerts.

Each time the roar would nearly fade, some Presley innovation would revive it. In the middle of a song, he would hold up his hand and stop everything while he hitched up his pants before picking up the frenzied pace once more. The crowd yelled its vocal support for his each and every move.

The MC had told us the performer was just 19 (he was actually 20, of course), and it stretched the imagination that one so young could have so much stage presence. At least one high school junior, attending the concert with his first heart-throb, who was destined to be his first heart-break, had a distinct feeling he was seeing show business history develop.

The youngster, raised with Hank Williams and Lefty Frizzell in his soul, didn't understand the new music, the new beat and only about half the lyrics. But he felt a connecting link with this guy dressed in blushing pink.

Perhaps it was because the singer was of the same generation, and maybe it was because he dared to be different. And it could have been because the singer led the youth's girl, from whom he had never been able to coax a goodnight kiss, to shriek, jump up and down and lose virtually all her inhibitions.

Elvis Presley was also his own MC, interrupting the pulsating music to exchange gags with Bill Black or to mock the country music he was

**A dramatic picture of Elvis playing to a full
house in 1955.**

supposed to be representing. He would introduce a song with, 'We call this song "Little Darlin', when you went away you broke my heart, but when you come back I'm gonna break your jaw!"' Then he would erupt into his own inimitable version of 'That's All Right, Mama' or 'Blue Moon of Kentucky'.

Poor Hank Snow never had a chance. When he walked onto the stage after 45 minutes of Elvis Presley, the crowd's energy had been sapped. There was nothing left for applause, requests or even the ordinary footpatting that goes with country music. Few in the audience would forget Elvis Presley or what happened to him in the following months – the national television appearances, the millions of records sold, the movies and the controversy caused by his non-conformist dress and rebellious manner. The stealing of the show at every stop on the tour did not escape the expert eyes of one particular man in attendance. Hank Snow, the man who had to follow the act, was at that time managed by Colonel Tom Parker. "

Upstaged or not, Hank Snow was happy to take his lion's share of the receipts – and at the end of the tour, Colonel Parker booked him out again with the same artists, including Elvis, for another week-long tour from 29 May to 3 June. Once more, Elvis, Scotty and Bill barely had enough time for a flying visit home to Memphis before taking to the road again. The killing pace was not only affecting the three men, but also their transport. As Scotty Moore recalls:

ELVIS PRESLEY - King of Western Bop

" THAT boy,," drawled Tex Ritter, " sure gits audiences worked up, and he sure gits himself worked up getting 'em worked up."

The object of cowboy Ritter's remarks was twenty-year-old Elvis Presley, who has risen to record fame in the space of a few months as a rocking-and-rolling hill-billy.

Presley's weird Western Bop has startled many more people besides the old-cowboy singers like Tex Ritter. It has startled adults, who hear nothing but a mumble-jumble cacophony when Elvis sings. But teenagers are ecstatic about Elvis. So ecstatic that they rip the seats from the floor and the shirts from his back.

Even without his personal appearances British buyers have made such Presley pressings as " Heartbreak Hotel " and " Blue Suede Shoes " into best-sellers. And it does Elvis good to see all these golden royalties rolling in.

He's riding the luxury train like a man who owns the railroad company. Almost every week he buys himself a new suit—and he keeps account of his wardrobe. He now owns, apart from an extensive wardrobe, a couple of extensive rainbow-hued Cadillacs, a station-wagon and a motor-cycle.

He has recently persuaded his father to retire—at the ripe retiring age of thirty-nine. And he has refurnished and decorated a home for his mother. He even designed some of the new furniture himself.

He's not ashamed of the fact that his family were poor people—too poor even to afford the price of a guitar. He realised this fact and determined to do something about it. Instead of sitting down in the shadow of self-pity and moaning about the fact that he couldn't buy

Presley, the windmilling warbler from Tupelo, Mississippi, flails his way through his songs with a maximum of effort.

29

" It was about that time that my Chevy finally gave out, so Elvis went and bought a 1951 Lincoln Continental. Bill wrecked that one. We were doing a date in Arkansas and a truck pulled out and he ran it under the truck and totalled the thing.

Then Elvis bought this 1954 Cadillac – and that one was burned up near Texarkana, Arkansas. What happened was the wheel bearing went out. But Elvis wasn't payin' no damn attention to the car and all of a sudden he realized it was on fire. We couldn't put it out. All we could do was open the trunk and throw our clothes and instruments out all over the road to save them! "

No such dramas could dampen Elvis' spirits, however, for the towns he was playing were now getting much bigger – as were the audiences. His fame was spreading across the whole South and when "Baby, Let's Play House" got top rating from both *Billboard* and *Cash Box* magazines, there was no doubt that the boy from Tupelo was hot in more ways than one!

Elvis was being particularly well received in Texas, where in the space of a week he travelled from Fort Worth to Abilene, Midland, Amarillo and Lubbock. Cecil Holifield, a record-shops operator and the promoter of the show in Midland, reported the event to *Billboard* magazine in these words:

" Elvis Presley is continuing to gather speed over the South. West Texas is his hottest territory to date and he is the teenagers' favorite wherever he appears. His original appearance in the area was in January with Tom Perryman to more than 1600 paid admissions. In February, with Hank Snow at Odessa, 20 miles from Midland, paid attendance hit over 4000.

On April 1 we booked only Elvis and his boys, Bill and Scotty, plus Floyd Cramer on piano and a local boy on drums for a rockin' and rollin' dance for teenagers and pulled 850 paid admissions. We are booking Elvis for May 31, heading his own show with Ferlin Huskey, the Carlisles, Martha Carson, J.E. and Maxine Brown and Onie Wheeler on a round robin starting at 7.30 p.m. in Midland and 8.30 p.m. in Odessa. Incidentally, our sales of Presley's four records have beat any

Opposite: **Another title for Elvis – the 1955 headline which would soon be shortened to just "The King".**

individual artist in our eight years in the record business. 99

(A "round robin" meant that the artists had to leap into their cars as
soon as they had finished performing at one spot and dash immediately
to the next with very little time allowed for any unexpected occurrences
such as a flat tyre or a traffic hold-up!)

Billboard also reported the results of the first Annual Country and
Western Popularity Poll run in May by Bobby Ritter of Radio Station
WTUP in Tupelo. Over 1000 postcards had been received from sixteen
states placing Elvis, the local boy, top of the list of ten vocalists. It was a

**Elvis the car-lover with three of his early
vehicles; and (opposite) surrounded by fans
at the wheel of his first Cadillac.**

moment to savour for the singer described by the DJ as "our own twenty-year-old fireball".

While he was performing in Lubbock, on his short Texas tour, Elvis also had the pleasure of seeing himself described in the press in the local parlance as "The King of Western Bop".

Opening the show that night in Lubbock was a local teenager for whom fate would also hold out a glittering, if tragically short-lived career as a rock star – a bespectacled guitar player and composer named Buddy Holly. Watching from the wings of the Cotton Club when he had finished, Buddy was mesmerized by Elvis' performance and found himself as moved and impressed as anyone else in the audience. He never forgot the influence that Elvis had upon him, and in September 1958, the year before his death in a plane crash, he spoke for fellow musicians everywhere – as well as millions of young people – when he said, "All of us who have succeeded in the rock 'n' roll field in recent years can thank Elvis Presley – for the importance he has given to our kind of music."

Buddy, of course, recorded several of Elvis' hits including "Good Rockin' Tonight" and "Blue Suede Shoes", but although Elvis in turn admired his contemporary from Lubbock and was saddened by his death, he never actually covered a Holly original.

Though it is true to say that by this time in 1955 Elvis had undoubtedly already made a big impression on the South with his new brand of music, there still remained the rest of America – and it was on this that he set his sights as the days of summer grew hotter still.

3 barnstorming the nation

Elvis, Scotty and Bill were on the road for almost all of June and July 1955, with D.J. joining them for a good many of the bookings in the larger cities. They crossed and re-crossed Tennessee, Arkansas, Oklahoma, Mississippi, Alabama and Florida – with the inevitable mad dash each weekend to Shreveport for *Louisiana Hayride*, for which Elvis still received $18 and the other two $12 each! Their week-day venues included police benefit concerts, night clubs, open-air picnics and even Air Force bases. Whatever the location, though, Elvis was now sure to sell two thousand tickets and more for any appearance.

As the temperatures grew ever higher in the sun-scorched region of the Gulf Coast of America where the little combo spent most of those two months, so the emotions of Elvis' female fans grew hotter still. And with them the tempers of some of their boyfriends, who saw in the young rock 'n' roller a threat to their own intentions. Others, to the contrary, found that Elvis had quite the opposite effect on their chicks.

Johnny Cash, the Arkansas-born singer whose discs Elvis so admired, first toured with his stablemate from Sun Records that summer, and had the opportunity to see this female frenzy at first hand. He remembers:

A montage of photographs of Elvis on the

road in the mid fifties.

Opposite: **Elvis could be a knock-out with both male and female fans — here he comforts a girl who has fainted at one of his concerts.**

66   Screaming was nothing new, of course. Frank Sinatra had the bobby soxers back in the 'forties, but that was all contrived. The girls in Elvis' audience just screamed spontaneously. They would cry and moan and some even wet themselves. But for the noise you could have heard the popping of orgasms in most of those halls!

    Elvis loved it all, and he really brought them on. In some places the girls would try and throw themselves at him on stage and he needed people to keep them off. 99

Johnny Cash says that Elvis also started getting love letters at this time; some thrown at him on the stage, others posted to the Elvis Presley Enterprises office in Memphis. The messages they contained were relentlessly similar – declaring the girls' undying love for the sexy young singer. Some, according to Cash, even confided: "You don't have to marry me, Elvis – just give me your baby!"

    Flattered though he was by this, Elvis was equally puzzled about the hatred that he seemed to generate in some boys. "There were always some guys around who wanted to take a crack at him because they thought he was trying to take their girls away from them," says Johnny Cash. "He wasn't afraid of them, though, because he could take care of himself. A few times I know he laid out guys who called him out after a show." But there were other boys who had reason to thank Elvis – for his performances apparently put many a young woman in the mood for love after the show!

    Elvis himself preferred to remain as enigmatic as possible about his affairs with women – though he never made any secret of how much he enjoyed their adulation. A few years later, he recalled:

Elvis with his fellow Sun recording artist, Johnny Cash.

66   Some of them would try and get up on the stage and I'd have to push them back with my foot. But sometimes I couldn't hold them back and they would get on the stage and start pulling at my clothes. Then I would have to get off quick, and they would have to hide me in a store or a filling station until things quietened down. There were times when I thought we would never get away from those girls – and there were times when we almost didn't and I had to go to hospital for treatment to cuts or bruises. 99

GIRLS SCREAM 'SAVE ELVIS!'

...as he battles with an angry husband

ELVIS PRESLEY

From JOHN THEOBALD, New York, Friday

ELVIS "The Pelvis" Presley, the rock 'n' roll idol of America, was in trouble.

And to Patrolman Walter Zalaznski standing outside a plush hotel in Toledo, Ohio, today it sounded like **BIG** trouble.

He could hear dozens of hysterical women all screaming the same thing:

"Save Elvis! Save Elvis!"

Grimly, Zalaznski and his fellow patrolman, Bill Kina, decided to try.

Inside the hotel they fought their way through a mob of hysterical sobbing, teenage girls.

"Hold on, Elvis," they shouted. "We'll get you out."

Then they found him ... pounding another man with his fists.

The police rescued the other man.

"What's it all about?" they asked. Elvis 21, told them.

Load of Fans

"There I am, sitting in the bar with a load of my fans when this guy walks up to me and says:

"'My wife carries a picture of you in her handbag but not one of me.'

"Then he socks me.

The police arrested the other man. Levis Balint.

Elvis said he did not want to press charges, but in court Balint was fined £3 10s. and gaoled for seven days for assault.

Zalaznski said later: "Elvis put up a really good fight. He could cuss as well as the other guy, too."

Kina said: "Presley's no slouch – he was really working-over that guy. He threw several good punches."

For more news of Elvis see "Live Letters" – Page 14.

Elvis also referred to his worst experience that summer while he was playing Jacksonville in Florida. It was the first riot he had caused – though it would prove to be far from the last.

❝ I walked out of this back door after the show and there were twenty or thirty screaming girls. They dived on me and shredded this new sports coat I had just bought. Also my shirt and pants and underwear. Before the police rescued me I was left with only one shoe and one sock. Everything else was gone – even a lot of skin. They had to put iodine on me in hospital – and because I'm allergic to iodine, I broke out in a rash! **❞**

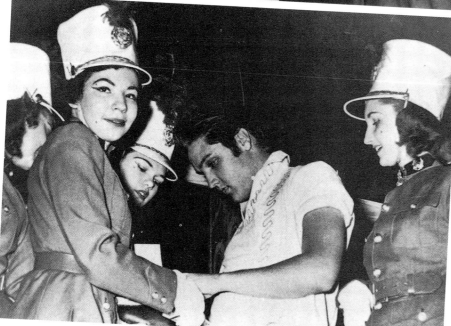

Posting with fans and giving autographs
following performances in Memphis.

In 1956 a Texas newspaper reporter challenged Elvis about the
reputation he had started to earn the previous summer as a womanizer.
Was it true, the newspaperman asked, that he had had "more girls than
Rabbie Burns"? At this, Elvis smiled and revealed the flash of wit that
was an integral part of his character and was to prove a handy weapon
later when dealing with over-inquisitive journalists.

" How would I know about that? How would anybody know
how many girls Rabbie Burns had? But Burns knew about love and his
verses prove it. Me? Maybe I know, too, but I don't have a great deal of
time. Girls are wonderful. Girls are the greatest, the mostest and

Opposite: Elvis with film starlet Natalie Wood, one of the best known of his early girlfriends.

loveliest! Anybody that says he doesn't like girls is missing his life. There wouldn't be anything without girls! **99**

It seems highly likely that Elvis left a number of broken hearts behind him as he journeyed across the southern states in 1955, for unlike later in his life he was then travelling relatively openly and the opportunity for romance was certainly there. If he was not actually on the road at night driving with Scotty and Bill, then Elvis generally stayed in inexpensive motels. There is ample proof that girls waylaid him in such places – and he was only human!

In the years since that summer there have been a number of somewhat sensational claims by young Southern belles to have slept with Elvis, and certainly several paternity suits were lodged against him. None of these instances has, however, been substantiated. So, if Elvis really was a "ram on the road", as some sources would like us to believe, the evidence still has to be produced. Certainly both Scotty and Bill, the two men closest to Elvis, have retained a discreet silence about his sex life during this hurly-burly ride to stardom. Scotty says:

Two more intimate snapshots of Elvis with mid-fifties girlfriends.

" Sometimes a girl would ride with us in the car, and Elvis would pet her. But he didn't like to go against his Ma and what she said about taking care of himself. He was always full of nervous energy, though, and we had to think of things to tire him out – like wrestling or pillow fights – so we could all get some sleep. Really, with all that travelling there just wasn't too much time for fooling about with women. "

Only Johnny Cash has added to this comment with an observation delivered with the hint of a twinkle in his eye. "Elvis had a project to see how many girls he could make," says Johnny, "he did okay!"

Despite all the excitement in which he now found himself caught up, Elvis never forgot to phone his mother in Memphis every day. Gladys and Vernon Presley had just a short while earlier moved into a single-storey new house in the appropriately named Getwell Avenue, and although there were many little jobs to keep them busy, neither could altogether stop worrying about their son out on the road.

D.J. Fontana has a particularly clear recollection of how attached Elvis was to his mother.

" Right from the start he used to call her every day, no matter where we were. Later, when the pressure started building, he'd call her two or three times a day. If it hadn't been for his mother, he probably wouldn't have made it. You remember when some of the papers got on to him for gyrating? They called it dirty. It seemed like every time we stopped he'd pick up a paper and there would be something attacking him. He took it pretty hard. So he'd call his mother and ask what he ought to do. She'd say, 'Now, Elvis, don't do anything you think is wrong or bad or let your fans down. If you know you're doing the right thing, then don't worry.' "

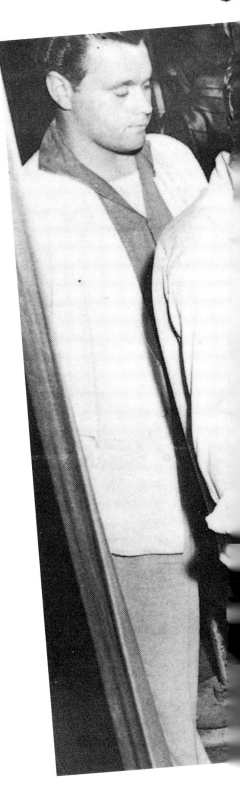

At home in Memphis, Elvis and a few friends get round the piano for an impromptu musical evening.

If this settled the young man's mind for a time, it did not stop him in
turn worrying about his mother, whose health was already starting to
decline despite the fact that she was only forty-three. He was relieved,
in fact, when at the end of July he was able to take a vacation and spend
two weeks in Memphis. They were relaxing and uninterrupted weeks,
made all the more pleasant when Bob Neal called on him with the news
that he had achieved another landmark in his career. The slow-starting
record "Baby, Let's Play House" had not only caught on in the South,
but had sold well enough to get into the national country music best-
seller charts.

This was Elvis' first disc to make a national listing – and as well as
reaching the number fifteen spot, it also earned a place at number eleven
on the chart of records most played by the nation's country disc jockeys.
The breakthrough towards national popularity had begun!

Reinvigorated by the rest, and well fed on his mother's indulgent
cooking, Elvis plunged back into a new round of activities in August.
First there was a new record to cut for Sam Phillips, and then a concert
in Memphis at which, for the first time, he would be the sole headliner.

Although Elvis was by now fairly familiar with the facilities at the
Sun recording studios on Union Avenue, cutting discs did not get any
easier for him. He never prepared for a session and, as was the case with

"That's All Right, Mama", what he finally got on tape was always a result of trial and improvisation. Marion Keisker, Sam's manager, who sat in the control room on all Elvis' sessions for the Memphis company, recalls vividly how long they all took.

    ❝   The first thing would be that Elvis would want to cover some record he had recently heard on the radio or else on a jukebox. So Sam would have to persuade him that was not a good idea – he had to come up with something that was new and different so that other people would copy *him*. ❞

Unlike most of the other Sun artists who became famous, such as Johnny Cash, Carl Perkins and Jerry Lee Lewis, Elvis did not write his own material, explains Marion.

A few quiet moments for Elvis on a river trip up the Mississippi on the cruise ship *Matsonia.*

❝   We either had to create something in the studio or get a song from someone else in our stable. And it was no good trying to give him something before he came into the studio and ask him to rehearse it. He just wouldn't do that. It was always the same: he'd come in and we'd all have to work over what was available until we found something that was right.   **❞**

This, in fact, was to be the pattern of recording that Elvis followed all of his life. And he was always quite frank about the fact that though it might not be everybody's ideal way of working, it was the *only* way for him. Talking some years later he said:

❝   For my recording sessions I work with ear musicians and not sheet musicians. They're great. You just hum or whistle or sing a tune for them once and then they get to work and inside a minute or two the joint is jumping.

But I always take my time to do the right thing. I can't properly explain it, but it all begins with listening, and more listening. It all narrows down gradually. I listen for hours. Then when I'm down to the songs I think I'll want to do, I'm ready. Me and the boys sometimes get together late at night and it's late morning before we call it a day.   **❞**

Elvis liked to get himself into the mood for recording; (*below*) Elvis, Scotty and D.J. go over some possible numbers to record; and (*right*) Elvis provides accompaniment for himself by beating on his guitar.

This method of working was, of course, by now almost second nature to Scotty and Bill, and neither of the two musicians complained as the hours in the small, stuffy studio dragged on and they seemed no nearer to making a record. Finally, on this occasion, failing to find anything he liked amongst the new material, Elvis began to play around with a song that had actually been Sun's first hit record – "Mystery Train", recorded by the black musician Little Junior Parker and his group, the Blue Flames.

This evocative rhythm and blues number had, in fact, been partly written by Sam Phillips in conjunction with Little Junior Parker – but as Sam sat at the control panel, he heard his words and melody transformed into something completely new and fresh. Here was a cover version that transcended its original and demonstrated – if such demonstration were needed – that Elvis now had a style that was uniquely his own.

Scotty and Bill again contributed immeasurably to the record's wailing, distinctive musical sound – but it was Elvis' voice that made it an instant classic. Although no one knew it at the time, "Mystery Train", Elvis' fifth record for Sun, was also to be his last for the company.

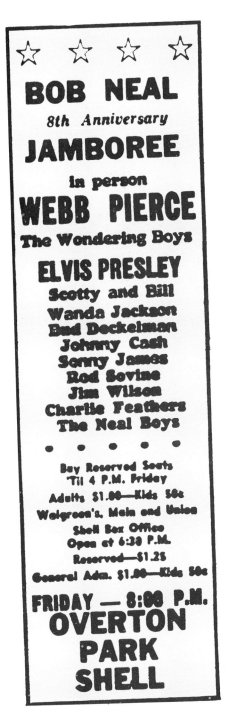

☆ ☆ ☆ ☆

BOB NEAL
8th Anniversary
JAMBOREE
in person
WEBB PIERCE
The Wondering Boys
ELVIS PRESLEY
Scotty and Bill
Wanda Jackson
Bud Deckelman
Johnny Cash
Sonny James
Rod Bovine
Jim Wilson
Charlie Feathers
The Neal Boys

• • • • •

Buy Reserved Seats
'Til 4 P.M. Friday
Adults $1.00—Kids 50¢
Walgreen's, Main and Union
Shell Box Office
Open at 6:30 P.M.
Reserved—$1.25
General Adm. $1.00—Kids 50¢

FRIDAY — 8:00 P.M.
OVERTON
PARK
SHELL

**Poster for Bob Neal's August 1955
Jamboree Concert in Memphis.**

Only one other song was laid down at that session: another country tune by Stan Kesler, the writer of Elvis' earlier number "I'm Left, You're Right, She's Gone". After his experience with that song, Sam Phillips decided that this new one, called "I Forgot to Remember to Forget", would make an ideal B side for "Mystery Train".

On Friday 5 August Elvis jumped on to the open-air stage of the Overton Park Shell in Memphis and played to the most enthusiastic audience of his life so far. Also on the bill were Johnny Cash, country singers Webb Pierce and Sonny James, and Wanda Jackson.

Elvis' appearance now warranted headlines and a photograph of the large crowds in his local newspaper, the *Memphis Press-Scimitar*, which carried the following report under the headlines

COUNTRY RHYTHM FILLS A CITY PARK

66   Overton Park Shell was jammed with an overflow audience last night for the wind-up of the Eighth Annual Bob Neal Country Music Jamboree Series.

Several hundred who wanted to hear in person Elvis Presley, Johnny Cash and Webb Pierce and some 22 other country music and comedy performers had to be turned away, while 4000 more lucky people enjoyed the show.   99

Although Bob Neal could take much of the credit for the staging of this concert, he was already in close contact with Colonel Tom Parker about Elvis' bookings for the coming months, as he has readily admitted.

66   The thing was I was involved in so many things in Memphis that I hadn't the time to go further afield. I had a popular local radio show and I was doing my promotions, and I just didn't want to be always going away from town and being on the road. So I got Colonel Parker involved because he was promoting shows nationally and would use Elvis on these tours. Once I had got the Colonel interested in him, I had a partnership with him for a while.

I was Elvis' manager for about a year I guess, but eventually I decided to drop out of the scene because I felt the boy was going to be a big hit.

In fact, practically all of 1955 there were negotiations going on with people who wanted to buy Elvis' contract from Sun Records. So he needed someone who knew his way around the music business to look after him. **99**

The influence Parker could wield was soon brought home to Neal when he was approached by the promoters of the prestigious Big D Jamboree country music show in Dallas, who wanted Elvis for their Saturday-night concerts held at the large Sportatorium.

Until now, the *Louisiana Hayride* promoters had kept Elvis to the letter of his exclusive contract – fee and all. But after some astute negotiating by the redoubtable Colonel it was agreed that the young singer could play the Big D Jamboree every fourth Saturday night. The delighted Dallas promoters thereafter redoubled their publicity push for the concerts – heralding Elvis as "one of the brightest new stars in the field with three records in the Top Ten Country Music Charts", as well as offering a free bus ticket home for all members of the audience who travelled by public transport!

The Colonel's mastery at publicity could also be sensed at work behind the increasing amount of coverage that Elvis was getting in newspapers, and more particularly the country music magazines such as *Country Song Roundup* and *Cowboy Songs*. Facts about his life were already being glamorized in building his image. Under a heading "Sun's Newest Star", an anonymous *Cowboy Songs* writer noted in one breathless piece of prose:

66   Lucky Elvis Presley is already enjoying the first reality of his life's dream – to sing for people and hear the spontaneous applause that means he's made a hit! When Elvis was a youngster down in Tupelo, Mississippi, folks used to stop him on the street and say, 'Sing for us, Elvis.' And he would . . . standing on the street corners in the hot Mississippi sun . . . or in church . . . or at school . . . anywhere someone wanted to hear him, he'd sing.

Now the same thing is happening all over again. When he's recognized on the street or at any public place, people call out, 'Sing for us, Elvis!' He has also been making personal appearances and bringing

Pages 91–96: A remarkable sequence of photographs following Elvis from his dressing room to a performance.

the house down every time. As the featured entertainer at the grand opening of a new business arcade, he played to a wildly enthusiastic audience of more than 3000 – who couldn't restrain themselves and started dancing and jitterbugging when Elvis sang 'That's All Right, Mama'. **99**

Someone who was among the throng of people who gathered for this opening at Katz Drug Store in Memphis was a pretty teenage brunette named Becky Yancey who was later to become Elvis' personal secretary when he and his family settled in the big mansion "Graceland" on the outskirts of the city. Referring to her first encounter with Elvis, Becky said recently:

66   I first met Elvis when my brother and I talked our parents into taking us to the grand opening of a new shopping centre. Elvis, Scotty Moore and Bill Black were playing from the back of a flatbed truck behind the Katz Drug Store.

The shopping centre was full of boys and girls when we got there. Elvis was wearing a pink shirt and tight black pants with a small patch on the bottom. His hair was combed back in the famous ducktail.

I was wearing a tight black skirt and pink sweater, and when I asked him for his autograph he said, 'Sure. But who do I sign this for, Marilyn Monroe?' Later I got a paper drinking cup and Elvis autographed it for me. I threw it away because my brother kidded me so much about it. However, I became a devoted Elvis fan that day. **99**

A rare moment of
relaxation for Elvis
in the garden of his
home in Memphis in
1955.

A golden future in his grasp — the handsome young rocker soon to have the world at his feet.

Elvis performing in the open air in Tupelo in 1956. Scotty Moore can be seen on the right.

An early publicity photograph of Elvis
showing him in country and western
clothes!

"The Hillbilly Cat" destined to become "The King of Rock 'n' Roll" in 1956.

Studio publicity photograph for Elvis'

first movie, *Love Me Tender*.

Elvis on the set of *Love Me Tender* which he filmed in 1956.

Mean, moody and magnificent – the
object of a million screams! One of
Elvis' own favourite photographs
from the fifties!

A typically ecstatic reception from Elvis'
female fans!

Memphis, in fact, was now becoming full of female fans, and the lucky ones might get a chance of a ride on the powerful Harley-Davidson motorbike Elvis had bought during his recent holiday and on which he loved to roar through the city streets. With a dark cap pulled over his eyes, he was the spitting image of his screen idol, Marlon Brando – and often aped him in manner and speech.

The increasing influence of Colonel Parker at this time also resulted in Elvis being lined up for the first time with a major star of popular music – a star whose part in the explosion of rock 'n' roll music has been widely acknowledged, Bill Haley. News of the combination of the two talents, the thirty-year-old Michigan-born band leader and the young rocker ten years his junior, was given in a typical announcement from the Colonel's Madison office under the headline "NEW POLICY COMBINES POPS AND C&W".

A panoramic view of one of Elvis' open air concerts in 1955.

 Colonel Tom Parker of Jamboree Attractions, one of the

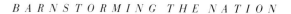

Elvis with his favourite Harley-Davidson motorbike, looking remarkably like his screen idol, Marlon Brando! (*Below*) With a Memphis fan; (*overleaf*) signing autographs; and pictured in Memphis with his friend, film star Nick Adams, riding pillion.

nation's major bookers and promoters of country and western talent, is instituting a new policy by presenting a combination of popular and country and western music in a one-nighter tour. Parker is teaming Bill Haley and His Comets with Hank Snow for an extended tour which will include Elvis Presley joining the tour in Oklahoma City. "

By the summer of 1955, Bill Haley was already well known throughout America for his hit records such as "Crazy, Man, Crazy", "Shake, Rattle and Roll" and "Rock Around the Clock", which later in the year was to be used as the theme song for the movie *The Blackboard Jungle* and thereafter make Haley a star all over the world. Haley, who died in 1981, talked revealingly in 1958 about his tour with Elvis – although it has to be said that the credit he accords to himself in the young singer's rise to fame is perhaps just a little overblown.

66   Elvis was just another kid with a guitar. Colonel Tom Parker wasn't his manager at that time; as I recall he was being handled by someone out of Memphis. Anyhow, around that time Parker became interested because Elvis had three or four small records and was playing through the South.

One day the Colonel called my manager, Lord Jim Ferguson, and said, 'Look, I've got this kid, I can't take him over, but I want him to get some experience, would you let me take him on tour with Bill?' And since my manager and Tom were good friends, he agreed. The tour was Hank Snow and myself and it was a regular one-nighter tour.

I remember when Presley came on the show. He was a big, tall, young

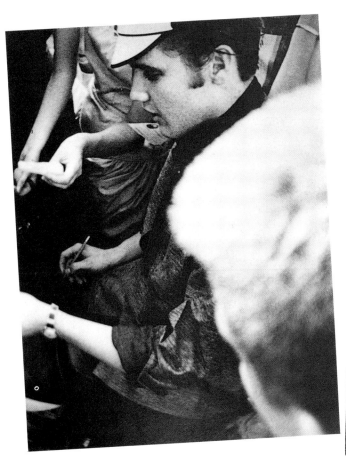

kid. He didn't have too much personality at that time. The first couple of nights I didn't catch his act. I think Hank Snow went on first, half an hour or so, and then we went on. We closed the show, naturally.

The first time I talked to Elvis was backstage as we were getting ready to go on. He came over to me and told me he was a fan of mine and we talked. He wanted to learn, which was the important thing. Then another night he went out and did a show and asked me what I thought.

I told him, 'Elvis, you're leaning too much on ballads and what have you. You've got a natural rhythm feeling, so do your rhythm tunes.' Now this was before he was a big hit, you know? So he went out and he had the attitude which most young kids do that he was really going to go out there and stop the show and knock Bill Haley off the stage – which at that time was an impossibility because we were number one. And he went out and he was facing Bill Haley fans, of course, and he couldn't do it.

The band leader Bill Haley, with whom Elvis appeared in 1955 and who claimed a considerable influence on the singer's career.

When I came off after doing my show I found him half-crying in his dressing room, very downhearted. So I sat down with him and told him, 'Look, you have got a lot of talent', and I explained a lot of things to him. He and I buddied together for about a week and a half after that until he left. I didn't realize just how big he was going to be, but once the Colonel got him his deal with RCA there was no stopping him. **99**

Though Elvis may well have benefited from his tour with Bill Haley, he was certainly far from just a kid with a guitar at this point in time. And newspaper reports of the Haley–Snow dates on which Elvis appeared clearly indicate that he got the sort of reception from the crowds that would hardly have left him downhearted and on the edge of tears! His audiences in the more northern states of Pennsylvania and Virginia might not have tried to tear the walls down like his fans in the South, but they certainly sat up and took notice and sent the sales of his records soaring.

During the month of September, Elvis, Scotty and Bill played a total of twenty-one shows in just twenty-four days, their itinerary taking them to places as far apart as Roanoke, Cleveland and St Louis. After just six weeks, "Mystery Train" had reached the top spot on the country music sales list, and was to remain in the charts for a record forty weeks – in fact, the longest period any Elvis record ever remained on any hit parade!

In that same month Elvis returned to Florida once again, where two more unexpected but significant events occurred. In Jacksonville, the town where he had experienced his first riot, he was now greeted by a group of local mothers who, aware of previous events, had protested to town hall officials about his act. Asked by the city council to be more restrained in his performance, Elvis responded by wiggling nothing more suggestive than his little finger – though even this provoked the usual barrage of screams. Speaking briefly to the press, he quietly justified his singing style in these words: "I don't think my actions on stage are vulgar. I know that I get carried away with the music and the beat sometimes, and I don't know quite what I am doing. But it is all rhythm and beat – it's full of life."

But if this action pacified the officials of Jacksonville, it did nothing to stop the question of his gyrations dogging his footsteps in the months which followed when preachers and critics also took up the hue and cry.

Something about which Elvis could not have had any inkling happened three nights later when he appeared at the Florida State Theater in Miami. For in the audience was a woman who was to have a very dramatic impact on his career. Her name was Mae Boren Axton, and she was a former publicist for Hank Snow. She was also a song writer, and currently working as a school teacher in the city.

Mae had seen Elvis earlier when he had first appeared on the Hank Snow show, and intrigued by all the stories of his roller-coaster ride towards success, booked herself a ticket for his performance. On the way to the theatre – so the legend goes – she passed a man slumped drunkenly against a street corner. Although he was almost unconscious, Mae heard him utter a phrase which rang through her head: "I'm so lonely I could die." The song writer in her told her that this was the raw material for a tune, and before the lights dimmed on Elvis' performance she had scribbled some lyrics on to the back of her programme.

Mae was deeply impressed by the range of Elvis' singing: from the raw power of "That's All Right, Mama" to the sentimental "You're a Heartbreaker". And as she looked again at the song she had written, she became convinced that this was the singer who could deliver the words with all the intensity and feeling they demanded.

Because of her connections, Mae had no difficulty in getting backstage after the performance and introducing herself to Elvis who was, as ever, the perfect gentleman. Without hesitation she thrust the song at Elvis and told him he should record it sometime. The title she had scribbled on the top of the page was "Heartbreak Hotel".

"He made chills run up my back, man" – singer Bob Luman.

October went by in a blur of engagements, though now the package in which Elvis travelled was being called the Elvis Presley Jamboree. Along with him were Johnny Cash, Floyd Cramer, Bobby Lord, Jimmy Newman and Jean Shepard. Again, he sold out dates across Texas from Abilene to Amarillo, thereafter playing St Louis from 21–23 October and rounding off the month at a giant country fair in Prichard, Alabama from 26–28 October.

At Prichard, another country artist named Bob Luman, resting between sets, saw Elvis in action for the first time, and later spoke admiringly of his impression of the boy who was billed around the fairground as "The Folk Music Fireball":

66 This cat came out with a sort of sneer on his face, and he stood behind the mike for five minutes, I'll bet, before he made a move. Then he hit his guitar a lick and broke two strings!

So there he was, these two strings dangling, and he hadn't done anything yet, and these high-school girls were screaming and fainting and running up to the stage. Then he started to move his hips real slow like he had a thing for his guitar. He made chills run up my back, man, like when your hair starts grabbing at your collar. 99

Elvis' astonishing impact was not only being experienced by his fans and other performers, but country music disc jockeys across the nation were also becoming increasingly impressed by his records, and on 2 November, at their thirtieth annual convention in Nashville, the DJs unanimously named him "Best New Male Singer". *Billboard* magazine similarly awarded him a scroll declaring him to be the "Most Outstanding New Artist of 1955" and the rival music magazine *Cash Box* matched this with their award as "Up-and-Coming Star of the Year".

Hardly had news of this trio of successes broken than a still bigger sensation was released to the press: Elvis was to leave Sun for a record fee and sign a new long-term contract with one of the biggest labels in America, RCA–Victor Records of New York. As Bob Neal intimated, moves to take Elvis to a major label had been going on for some while, but it was Colonel Tom Parker who finally saw the deal through after intense competition between Columbia Records, Atlantic Records and RCA.

Mitch Miller, the legendary head of Columbia Records, had been one of the first national bosses to spot Elvis' potential, but when an asking price of $20,000 was mentioned, Mitch felt this was too high a sum to risk on an artist who had still to capture a nationwide audience. Next, Ahmet Ertegun, president of the famous rhythm and blues label Atlantic Records, was willing to go as high as $25,000 for Elvis' signature, but backed out when Colonel Parker insisted he was looking for a figure almost double that!

That left RCA–Victor, then the leading maker of country and western records in the USA, who saw Elvis fitting neatly into this category. As they were already the label of two of Colonel Parker's other stars, Hank Snow and Eddy Arnold, the prospects seemed favourable – but understandably the men in New York were more than a little concerned about the huge investment they were being asked to make: $35,000 for the Sun contract and a $5000 bonus for Elvis in lieu of his royalties from the Memphis company. No artist before had *ever* been considered worth such a signing-on fee – but that is precisely what the canny ole Colonel negotiated for his client. It was, as one writer later put it with a prophetic turn of phrase, equivalent to a king's ransom.

In a press release dated 22 November, both sides involved in the deal were enthusiastic, if a little cagey.

66   Elvis Presley, 20, Memphis recording star and entertainer, has been released from his contract with Sun Record Co of Memphis and

Elvis Presley   Hank Snow

Homer & Jethro   Jim Reeves

RCA began their promotion of Elvis as a country and western artist! He was also shown as such on early collections of his songs.

A Victor...

best brand in Country and Western music!

With the world's greatest artists, the leading label in the great C&W field is

y Arnold · Chet Atkins · Don Gibson

d Cramer · Sons of the Pioneers · Del Wood

Jimmy Driftwood · Roy Rogers and Dale Evans · Porter Wagoner · Skeeter Davis · The Browns

Johnnie & Jack · Hank Locklin · Blackwood Brothers

ELVIS PRESLEY
COUNTRY HITS

SOUTHERN MUSIC PUBLISHING CO. LTD.
sole selling agents MUSIC SALES LTD. 78, Newman Street, London W1E4.

will record exclusively for RCA–Victor, it was announced today by Sam C. Phillips, Sun President.

Phillips and RCA officials did not reveal terms, but said the money involved is probably the highest ever paid for a contract release for a country-western recording artist.

'I feel Elvis Presley is one of the most talented youngsters today,' Phillips said, 'and by releasing his contract to RCA–Victor we will give him the opportunity of entering the largest organization of its kind in the world, so his talents can be given the fullest opportunity.'

Negotiations were handled by Col. Tom Parker of Jamboree Attractions, Madison, Tenn.; Bob Neal, Presley's personal manager; and Steve Sholes, head of RCA–Victor's artist and repertoire department in Nashville. **"**

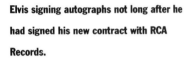

Elvis signing autographs not long after he had signed his new contract with RCA Records.

Despite the obvious fact that Sam Phillips himself might have gone on to share in the millions that Elvis later made, had he retained his contract, he has remained unshakable in the belief that he took the right decision. Sun Records were never going to be big enough to cope with the demand that developed for Elvis' records, he says, and he himself wanted to be free to pursue the line that had always driven him – seeking out new talent.

Steve Sholes, who had committed his company to Elvis' future at what seemed like an astronomical cost, was a genial forty-five-year-old talent spotter who had already landed an impressive roster of stars for RCA. He was the man taking what observers saw as the real gamble – though he himself was already sure in his own mind of the young star's potential. A few years before his death in 1968, Steve talked frankly about the decision that put Elvis' career into overdrive and brought RCA–Victor their biggest-ever star.

66   When the deal was agreed I crossed my fingers and prayed, and thank heavens I was right! I had been watching Elvis' career for some time but it was still one hell of a risk for us.

Actually, I'll never forget the first time I heard him sing. One of our representatives sent me a copy of his first Sun record, 'That's All Right, Mama'. I had been looking for something, I didn't know what – it was a sound or a beat – and I'd been looking for it for a long time. When I played that record, I knew I'd found it. But when I called Sun Records I was really disappointed to find he had already signed a contract with them. After that I just had to sit and be patient. **99**

Elvis himself scarcely had time to think about all the bargaining that had been taking place on his behalf. He, Scotty and Bill were on the road fulfilling engagements in Tennessee and Mississippi. By a curious twist of fate, among the artists on the tour was Carl Perkins, a guitarist, composer and singer whom Sam Phillips had already signed to the Sun label and was hoping to promote as the successor to Elvis. In fact, within a month of the deal which took Elvis to RCA–Victor, Carl had composed and recorded for Sam what was to prove his greatest hit, "Blue Suede Shoes". In 1956, Elvis was to cover this same number with even greater success for his new company. Recently, Carl reflected on those extraordinary days in both their lives.

66 Elvis and I went back a long way – we were poor boys together. We shared the same record label for a time and we even went out on those little package shows which Bob Neal booked. You could pay a dollar and see Elvis, Johnny and me all on the same bill! In some places, if you were twelve or under it cost you nothing!

All we did really was take country music and colour it up – that was our style of rock 'n' roll. Elvis was a phenomenal guy, though. Nobody swung a guitar like him – he used it as if it was an extension of his body.

That boy had everything. He had the looks, the moves, the manager and the talent. And he didn't look like Mr Ed like a lot of us did. In the way he looked, the way he talked, the way he acted – he really *was* different. **99**

And referring to his famous song, Carl added:

66 I wrote 'Blue Suede Shoes', which both Elvis and I had huge hits with, and you know, it was the easiest song I ever wrote. I got up at 3 a.m. one morning with this idea in my head, seeing kids by the bandstands so proud of their new city shoes. I went downstairs and wrote out the words on a potato sack – we didn't have any reason to have writing paper around! 99

There was just time before Christmas for Elvis to return to Memphis for a photograph session to mark his new deal with RCA in which he was pictured with Steve Sholes, his proud mother and father, and an understandably beaming Colonel Parker. There were also moments for him to reflect on where all his "barnstorming the nation" – as *Cash Box* magazine had vividly described his recent months of activity – had led him. Certainly, he and his parents could look forward to a very happy Christmas and an even more prosperous New Year.

The holiday season was also marked by a touching reunion with someone from Elvis' past, when his former school teacher at Humes High School, Mrs Mildred Scrivener, invited him to return as a guest to the school's Christmas variety show. It had been on this self-same show back in December 1952 that Elvis had nervously entertained his fellow pupils with a version of "Cold, Cold, Icy Fingers".

When he repeated the number in the inimitable style which was now arousing the nation's teenagers, the pupils who had become his successors as well as his fans roared their approval until the very rafters of the assembly hall resounded.

Elvis could look forward to a really prosperous 1956 . . .

4 the king of rock 'n' roll

The raw emotion of Elvis recording in 1956.

The RCA–Victor recording studios in Nashville, Tennessee into which Elvis, Scotty and Bill walked after the 150-mile journey from Memphis on the afternoon of 10 January 1956 were, surprisingly, not that much larger or grander than those at Sam Phillips' Sun Records.

Elvis, though, was feeling in great form. He had enjoyed Christmas at home with his folks in their comfortable new bungalow, and they had given him a splendid twenty-first birthday party two days earlier with a few of his friends and relatives. From scraping around to earn a few dollars playing on the back of flatbed trucks, as he had been doing just over a year earlier, he was now an increasingly confident stage performer and recording star, with all the resources of a big label ready to push him towards the stardom he dreamed about. (Already, in fact, RCA had reissued "Mystery Train" and soon after would re-release the earlier four Sun discs.) And in Colonel Parker, Elvis sensed he had a mentor who was planning a bright and lucrative future for him.

It had given Elvis a sense of satisfaction to return as a sought-after artist to Nashville – known far and wide as "Music City" because of the conglomeration of music companies and recording studios that peppered the town – because of his unhappy experience while playing the Grand Ole Opry in September 1954 when, apart from the indifference of the audience, the manager Jim Denny had suggested he might be better off returning to truck driving. The RCA studios were located at 1525 McGavrock, in a squat and rather unattractive two-storey building which actually belonged to the Tennessee Methodist TV, Radio and Film Commission.

The recording studios were situated at the rear of the building behind a suite of offices. The facilities, by today's standards, were primitive indeed: a studio for the musicians that was crowded with anything over a dozen people in it; a control room that was equally cramped when more than four people sat down; and at the back, a stairwell that

An informal
picture of Elvis
and Scotty
during a
recording
session.

doubled as somewhere to get a breath of fresh air between takes, and sometimes as an echo chamber!

At the foot of these stairs stood a soft-drinks machine, and it was said that if anyone used this piece of equipment while a recording session was in progress the sound could be heard on the tape. For Elvis, however, this rudimentary echo chamber was to help provide the unique sound for the greatest of the five songs that were to emerge from his first session in the studios.

Elvis' music had, of course, been refined over the course of 1955 from a raw mixture of country and rhythm and blues to the kind of hard-driving, up-beat music that was apparent on singles like "Mystery Train". Steve Sholes and RCA, however, were looking for something still more stylized and closer to pop – the pure Elvis Presley sound that had been hinted at but not yet quite delivered on the Sun records. On the advice of the experienced recording chief of RCA in Nashville, thirty-two-year-old Chet Atkins, himself a superb guitarist and popular recording star, more personnel were added to the previous Sun line-up of just Elvis, Scotty and Bill.

D.J. Fontana, with his wealth of experience of Elvis on the road, was a natural for the drums. Similarly, Floyd Cramer, who had worked with him live on numerous occasions, was brought in to play the piano. Chet Atkins decided to sit in himself as an added guitar, and for the first time Elvis had a backing group in the shape of the top country and gospel band, the Jordanaires (Gordon Stoker, Ben Speer and Brock Speer).

Elvis Presley – drummer! Another informal picture taken in the RCA studios in Nashville.

Shortly after 2 p.m. on that cold January afternoon, Elvis warmed up on a classic rhythm and blues number, "I Got a Woman", penned by the famous blind musician Ray Charles. Once again, Elvis took a familiar tune and rendered it in his own unique way.

Outstanding though "I Got A Woman" was, it was immediately superseded when Elvis took up the strains of "Heartbreak Hotel", Mae Boren Axton's song which he had been carrying in his music portfolio ever since their meeting in Miami. Chet Atkins, who had already studied the music and lyrics, decided that a minimum of accompaniment was needed on this stark and painful number, and dropped himself from the line-up. He also felt that the stairwell "echo chamber" would enhance the feeling of loneliness in the lyrics, and

Jordanaires Join Elvis

Jordanaires During A Recording Session

The Jordanaires team up once again with Elvis to start a new movie.

Gordon Stoker, of th.. Jordanaires, dropped us a note from Hollywood to say they were going to Puerto Rico for a short vacation and to attend the Columbia Records convention.

Elvis' new picture will be put ut by MGM and will be, Natural-

ly, a musical. The name of the movie will be "Viva Las Vegas". Starring as Elvis' leading lady will be the lovely Ann Margaret.

This picture will undoubtedly be a huge success as all of Elvis' pictures are. These are the kind of pictures the whole family can enjoy. For the vast audience of music lovers there will be seventeen wonderful new songs.

While waiting for this picture

to be released, if you haven't already done so, be sure and listen to RCA Victor's current LP album It Happened At The World's Fair. It features the music sound track of the picture. Ask your RCA Victor dealer about the beautiful color photo made available in conjunction with the RCA Victor LP album "It Happened At The World's Fair".

Two of the flood of newspaper and magazine articles that charted every move in Elvis' spectacular rise to stardom.

arranged for its use. These very basic, but none the less important decisions were undoubtedly crucial in the making of "Heartbreak Hotel" – as well as the way in which Elvis flung himself with almost demonic energy into singing the tune that afternoon.

At 5 p.m. the musicians in the studio took a break, returning later for a further session when one more song was laid down: a storming cover version of Clyde McPhatter's 1953 hit "Money Honey" by Jesse Stone. These two sessions left Elvis limp and sweating, and he sighed with relief when Chet Atkins called an end to recording at 10 p.m.

Elvis slept deeply that night and well into the following day, returning to the studios at 4 p.m. to cut two further songs: "I'm Counting on You" by Don Robertson, on which Scotty Moore gave a fine performance on lead guitar, and 'I Was the One' by Aaron Schroeder, Hal Blair and Claude Demetrius, which contained some outstanding piano playing by Floyd Cramer. By 7 p.m. it was a satisfied group of musicians – Elvis included – that left the McGavrock studios, convinced that they had made some good records, though little realizing that they had also made history.

Steve Sholes was a relieved man. He said later:

66 There were people in the music business then who reckoned I was a fool. They reckoned I'd never be able to get Presley sounding the way he had with the Sun label. Those early records had a raw and rough edge to them. Well, we didn't get the same sound. Elvis' own style had evolved since his Memphis days. We rode along with it.
     The only problem we had with Elvis was the fact he held his guitar close to his face and played it so loudly you couldn't hear his voice over the mike. We had to give him a felt pick, but even so he'd still break a string every two or three takes. He was always wanting to do a song again because he thought he could do it better – and when you get that kind of dedication in an artist you *know* he is going to be successful. 99

Floyd Cramer later spoke for all the musicians.

66 It was great working with Elvis because we all had the same idea about music – to keep it simple with no technical exhibitionism. Like me, he believed in getting his feeling across as directly as possible. For this reason he would take all the time he needed to do it. 99

Chet Atkins also remembered the session, but for a rather different reason.

66 Elvis came in dressed in pink pants with blue stripes and he was really nice. He said, 'Yes, sir' and 'No, sir' until it was excessive – maybe even too respectful.
     While he was singing his pants ripped because of all his shaking about. So someone went out and bought him another pair before he left. Elvis threw the old pair in a corner. A girl working for the Methodist Publishing Company in the same building saw the pants and asked me

what she should do with them. I told her to take good care of them, since the boy was going to be famous.

I don't think she believed me, but she kept the pants anyway. Six months later she went on the TV show *I Have a Secret* with Elvis' pants! **99**

By the following day, 12 January, Elvis was on the road once again with Scotty and Bill to join up with Hank Snow for a week-long tour of Texas. He sold out at San Antonio and Fort Worth, where his audiences were almost wholly teenagers. Poor old Hank Snow, seeing this, realized that he and Elvis could no longer share the same bill: their audiences were worlds apart.

During these same early days of January, Colonel Parker had also been busy on the next phase of Elvis' career – to reach the whole USA at one fell swoop via television. It would take the boy a great deal longer to cover the nation through its theatres than over the medium of the TV screen, he reckoned.

Now that Elvis had a growing reputation there would be no need for an audition, and so the Colonel skilfully negotiated six Saturday-night appearances for him on the half-hour CBS series *Stage Show* featuring the Tommy and Jimmy Dorsey big band and produced by Jackie Gleason in New York.

Elvis had been sold to the show – which was then doing rather poorly in the ratings war – as "a guitar-playing Marlon Brando" (a term that delighted him), and not only did he pick up a fee of $1250 per show, but also got to plug his first RCA release, "Heartbreak Hotel". His first appearance on *Stage Show* on 28 January and what it did for the show's popularity as well as Elvis' rise to fame is now as much a part of music lore as the record he had just cut in Nashville. The nation's viewers from coast to coast sat back in open-mouthed amazement as the boy from Memphis electrified the screen with his remarkable voice and bumping, grinding movements. No one had *ever* seen anything like it before!

D.J. Fontana, furiously pounding his drums in accompaniment, still remembers the time very well.

"   The Dorsey programme was the first big television show we had done – and were we scared to death! After all, we were just a bunch of hillbillies going to New York. We drove up, working shows on the way up, and then on our way back down. After that, of course, the TV people treated Elvis like a king. They knew he could take their ratings from nothing to the top! **"**

Once again Elvis had the pleasure of storming a town that had previously rejected him. On his second visit a week later, New York's teenagers were out in force to squeal their ecstasy both inside and outside the CBS studios, and a doorman there uttered what many another harassed official at an Elvis appearance was later to exclaim: "I've never seen anything like it!" The star from the South was now becoming the sensation of the North as well, and once "Heartbreak Hotel" hit the record shops it was to be only a matter of time before Elvis had his first Pop Top Ten hit.

In many accounts of Elvis' life, the release of "Heartbreak Hotel" and his national exposure on television are portrayed as the watersheds in his career. From those January days, say the reports, Elvis was a superstar. But in fact he wasn't *quite*. Scotty Moore provides a more accurate and actually rather more interesting version.

Two rare pictures from Elvis' first major television appearance on the CBS series *Stage Show* in 1956.

❝ We really didn't know what was happening. We were on the road nearly every day – pulling into one town, putting on a show, and then back into the car and moving on to the next place. They told us the record was going well, but we'd heard that before and even if it was, we weren't getting any money from it. There was a lot of crowd reaction, of course, but we'd been seeing that for a year. How were we to know? We didn't even see any newspapers, and there wasn't much radio at night. ❞

Elvis was by then such a show stealer that other stars were being listed as the "added attractions" that he had once been – that is, if they were prepared to share the same bill with him. Indeed, as momentum built up over the spring months, the acts that had to endure the chants of "We

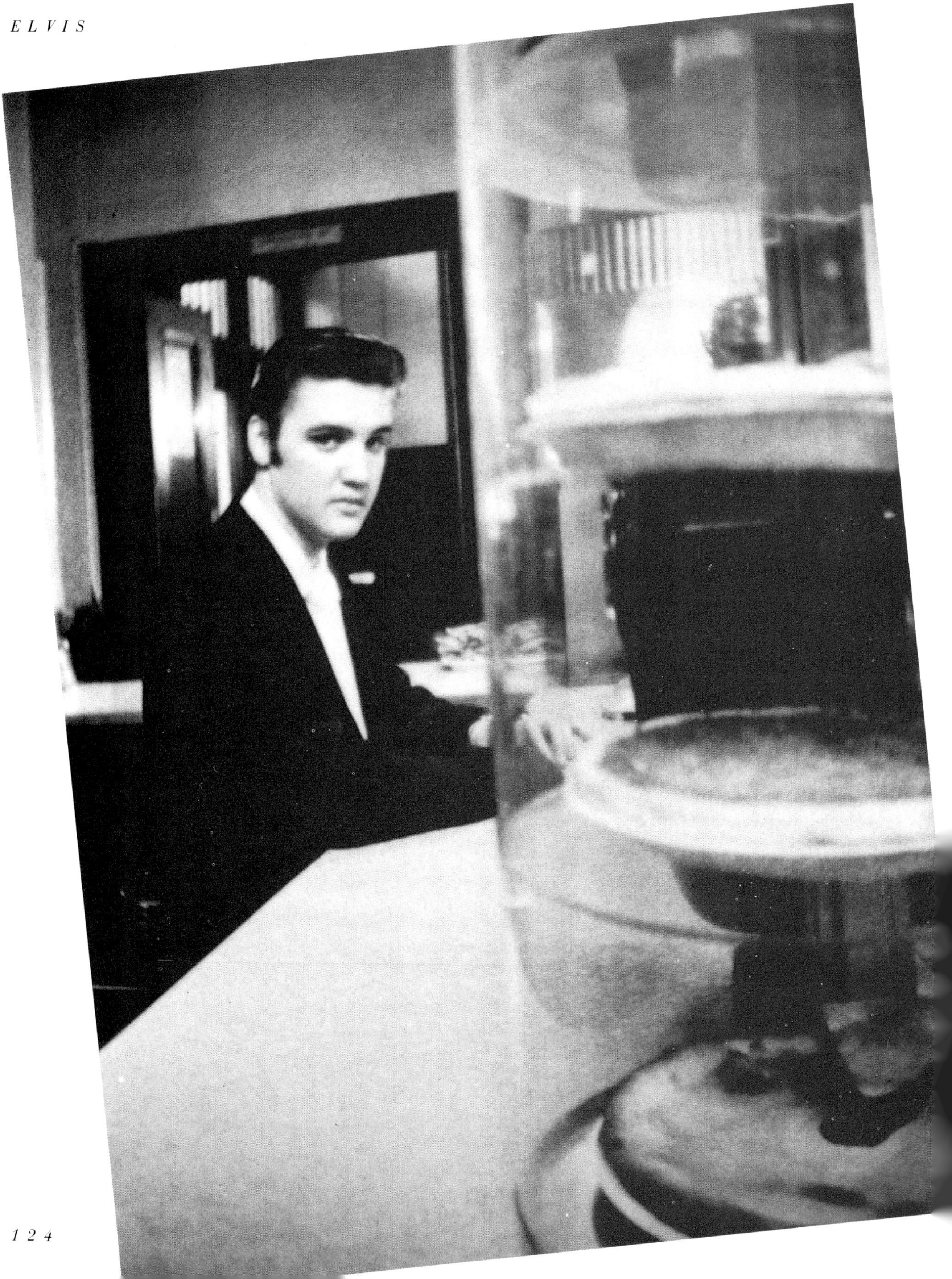

**Almost continually on the road in the early
months of 1956, Elvis was hardly aware of
the enormous fame that was beginning to
build up around him.**

want Elvis" before the star made his
appearance grew ever more strange:
in San Diego, for instance, he was
preceded by a female vocalist, an acrobatic
dance team and a xylophone player!

As the bookings for Elvis took him ever further afield, it became
necessary for him and the boys, Scotty, Bill and D.J., to abandon the
road and fly to some dates – especially the Dorsey shows in New York.
Elvis had always been nervous of aircraft, and a narrow escape in one of
them at this time confirmed his anxieties and very nearly nipped his
new-found stardom in the bud.

Elvis never liked talking publicly about the incident, but he did reveal
the facts to another singer, Roy Orbison, who also recorded for Sun and
had Bob Neal as a booking agent. Though the Texan-born singer of such
hits as "Crying" and "Only the Lonely" never toured with Elvis, they
did meet in Memphis in the mid 'fifties and knew each other well for a
number of years. Recently, Roy said of Elvis:

66   We were good friends, and his personality was very much like my own. We were both very nervous about going on stage – in fact, Elvis was more nervous than I was. Once we were on, it was OK. But what he was most afraid of was flying, and all because of a terrifying little incident that nearly ended his career in a few seconds.

Elvis told me he was in a two-engine charter plane with Scotty, Bill and D.J. flying to Nashville for a recording date. Suddenly, one of the engines failed. And then other troubles started to develop at the same time.

It was obvious that the plane would have to come down in a hurry, and the pilot was fortunate enough to find a deserted airstrip close at hand. I dread to think what would have happened if that other engine hadn't held out. Elvis told me he was petrified and could think only to pray, which he did until they landed safely. After that he was scared stiff of flying for years and only did so on rare occasions. 99

Elvis' stage act was condemned as "disgusting" and his singing "an unutterable bore" in a series of attacks which were made on him in 1956.

Although Elvis never completely lost this
nervousness over flying (and his anxiety was not
helped by the death of Buddy Holly in a plane crash
in 1959), much later in 1975 he did buy himself a
Corvair 880 Jet which he remodelled without
windows in the passenger area and filled with every
kind of distraction. For good luck, he named the
aircraft after his only child, Lisa Marie.

Roy Orbison also heard from Elvis about how he felt when, following
his TV appearances, critics from all sections of American society began
attacking what some of them considered his "disgusting" performances.
As Roy recalls:

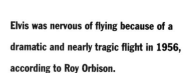

**Elvis was nervous of flying because of a
dramatic and nearly tragic flight in 1956,
according to Roy Orbison.**

66   When he started, he had to live down a lot of adverse
publicity, and most of that publicity was untrue. When you are the first,
which Presley was, then you're there to be picked on. He had to live

down that bad publicity by being a nice person. It rubbed off on him, in fact, and made him an even finer boy.   **,,**

However, "a fine boy" was certainly not what some of his detractors were calling him in those early months of 1956.

The first major attack on Elvis was delivered by the *New York Times'* television critic, Jack Gold.

,,   Mr Presley has no discernible singing ability. His specialty is rhythm songs which he renders in an undistinguished whine; his phrasing, if it can be called that, consists of the stereotyped variations that go with a beginner's aria in the bathtub. For the ear he is an unutterable bore . . .

From watching Mr Presley it is wholly evident that his skill lies in another direction. He is a rock-and-roll variation of one of the most standard acts in show business: the virtuoso of the hootchy-kootchy. His one specialty is an accented movement of the body that heretofore has been primarily identified with the repertoire of the blonde bombshells of the burlesque runway.   **,,**

The critic of the *Times'* rival newspaper, the *New York Journal-American*, Jack O'Brien, delivered an equally stinging attack on Elvis which concluded, "He can't sing a lick and makes up for his vocal shortcomings with the weirdest and plainly planned, suggestive animation short of an aborigine's mating dance."

The powerful Hollywood gossip columnist Hedda Hopper similarly took up O'Brien's accusation that Elvis – "Sir Swivel Hips" she called him – planned these gyrations. She had equally seen him, she reported, "rolling around on the stage with his arms and legs wrapped around the microphone as though they were bride and groom. At the crucial point, from my front row seat, I saw him give his bandsman a broad wink that spoke volumes." Miss Hopper also added, "Even when he is standing, every muscle jerks as though he were a marionette. I've seen performers dragged off to jail for less."

Next it was the turn of churchmen to attack Elvis. The Catholic Reverend William Shannon told his congregation, "Presley and his voodoo of frustration have become symbols in our country", while the Episcopalian Reverend Charles Graff used similar imagery in calling Elvis a "whirling dervish of sex". Billy Graham, the internationally famous evangelist, even added his voice to the growing hysteria when he was quoted as saying, "From what I've heard, I'm not so sure I want my children to see him."

City officials in a number of towns and cities where Elvis appeared accused him of "sexually setting young American womanhood on fire", and of encouraging young hoodlums to riot. This rioting, the *New York Daily News* went further, could be seen taking place from "puritanical Boston to julep-loving Georgia". In New York, a group of mothers taking a lead from their sisters in Jacksonville got up a petition to have Elvis banned from appearing on television. Some other towns even went as far as stopping local disc jockeys from playing Elvis' records and refusing permission for the holding of concerts where any kind of rock 'n' roll was to be played. A few DJs, perhaps believing that Elvis' popularity would be short-lived – or otherwise genuinely disliking his music – took to destroying Presley discs on the air and informed listeners that they were dedicated to eliminating what they called "wreck and ruin artists". Those in all sections of the media who wanted to be most directly abusive called the boy from Memphis, "Elvis the Pelvis".

Elvis himself maintained a remarkable calm through all these attacks, perhaps protected from the worst of them by his hectic schedule. He did, however, continue giving interviews to both newspapermen and disc jockeys, answering their accusations as best he could.

In one fascinating interview with Gordon Sinclair of the *New York Star*, Elvis revealed how much he hated the term "Elvis the Pelvis", which he thought was "the most childish expression I have ever heard".

Sinclair asked him bluntly, "Many parents seem to feel that you are a menace, evil and wicked, and the personification of easy money – how do you feel about that?" Elvis was equally blunt in his reply.

❝ Sir, I know they feel that way. Lots of them do. And I wish they didn't. I wish I could have a chance to sit down and talk to those parents because I think I could change their minds and their viewpoint.

Ever since I got to be a sort of name I've examined my conscience and asked myself if I led anybody astray even indirectly, and I'm at peace with my conscience. I don't drink and I don't smoke and I don't swear.

I read my Bible, sir, and this is no story just made up for now. My Bible tells me that what a man sows he will also reap and if I'm sowing evil and wickedness it will catch up with me. I'm right sure of that, sir, and I don't think I'm bad for people. If I did think I was bad for people I would go back to driving a truck, and I really mean this. **99**

In another discussion with TV chat show host Hy Gardner, Elvis dismissed some scandalous rumours from certain sections of the press that he had once shot his mother and that he smoked marijuana in order to work himself up into a frenzy! Elvis said:

66 Well, sir, I tell you, you've got to accept the bad along with the good. I've been getting some very good publicity, the press has been real wonderful to me, and I've been getting some bad publicity – but you have got to expect that and I know I have been doing the best I can. **99**

Elvis' respectful nature and lack of aggression with other people, whatever their intentions towards him, was eventually to calm and then win over those who had first seen him as some kind of Lucifer figure bent on corrupting youth. As so often before in history, he was a phenomenon who had come along at a convenient moment to have some of the nation's most obvious problems heaped on his shoulders. The young, it was said, were in a state or rebellion and looking for an identity, and Elvis was seen as an outrageous symbol of this upheaval.

The members of Elvis' family were naturally quick to defend him, Vester Presley, his father's brother, speaking for them all in his quiet, reasoned way.

66 Not everyone takes to Elvis when he first starts singing. Some say his act is vulgar. Some say he was no talent and he'll never last. Then there are those who don't say anything. They just raise their eyebrows, shake their heads, and wonder who he thinks he is and what does he think he is doing? But the young people agree that he is definitely not vulgar, has talent, and will certainly last forever. They could not care less about who he thinks he is or what he thinks he's doing.

As to what he thinks he's doing, whatever it is they like it. As to who he is, he's Elvis. That's all they know and it's all they will ever really need to know. They love him and he loves them. **99**

There were actually some adults who had expressed their support for Elvis, as he mentioned in another interview.

66 They have come to me and said, 'I don't personally like your kind of music, but my children like it and if they like it, I can't really kick about it because when we were young *we* liked the Charleston which *our* parents disliked.' That's being intelligent, I think. They're not running young people down just for having a good time. **99**

Probably the most dramatic of all the changes of opinion which later occurred among Elvis' critics was that of Hedda Hopper who, in 1963, confessed:

66 I was one of those who felt Elvis was a menace to young people who imitated him without realizing what they – or he – were doing. But I've seldom been more mistaken about anybody in my life.

He's actually a polite and very dedicated person. He's one of the new faces in our industry who has been promoted into a living legend, and we need dream stuff like Elvis to survive. **99**

Elvis was not yet a living legend in 1956, but in March he was having some difficulty surviving the killing pace of engagements set for him. On one occasion, after leaving a *Stage Show* appearance in New York, he drove through a snow storm to Los Angeles, moved on to San Diego and then to Denver. By the time he and his three musicians reached Jacksonville, Florida – the scene of earlier significant events – he was so exhausted that he collapsed and had to be rushed into hospital. This time, it was no performance to win a co-star's affections.

Elvis is given a hero's welcome when he
returns home. (*Above*) In Memphis he is
greeted by the King and Queen of the Cotton
Bowl Carnival; and (*below*) he revisits his
birthplace, Tupelo, with his mother and
father.

Tupelo officials present Elvis with a guitar to mark his achievements, while a fan offers him a cap!

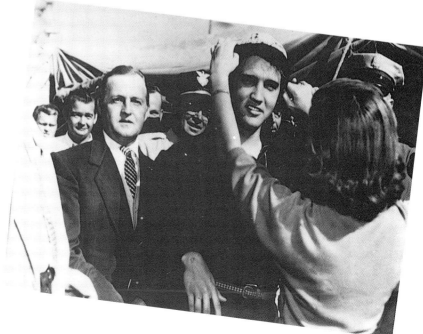

Despite the doctor's orders that he should rest, Elvis quit the hospital the following morning and went right on with his schedule. Later he said, "I was over-exhausted. One doctor told me that if I didn't slow down a little, I might have to lay off for maybe a couple of years. He said I was doing more work in half an hour on stage than a labourer does in a whole working day."

It was quite evident that Elvis could not continue at this pace. Colonel Parker, who had been busy engineering Elvis' ride to stardom, now felt the moment was right to become the boy's sole manager rather than sharing the responsibility with Bob Neal. Neal, for his part, was quite happy to relinquish control, and on 15 March the partnership which still rates as one of the most famous in show business was sealed.

"My contract with Elvis was up and I simply let it go," Bob explained straightforwardly. "I suppose I could have negotiated something for myself but I didn't. It was just the best thing for everybody."

Just over a week later, "Heartbreak Hotel" reached the number one spot on the American pop top ten. In all, this disc was to stay twenty-seven weeks in the charts – eight of them at the very top – confirming the Presley explosion on to the music scene.

The earliest publicity photographs of Elvis released in Britain in 1956 attempted to portray him as a kind of beef-cake singer!

The record also created another landmark for Elvis when it became the first disc to be released outside America – first of all in Great Britain, where it was put into the shops at the end of February. Elvis was, of course, practically unknown across the Atlantic, and even the UK distributors, HMV records, hedged their bets when they announced the release in an advertisement in the music press which read: "Take a dash of Johnnie Ray, add a sprinkle of Billy Daniels and what have you got? You have Elvis Presley, whom the American teenagers are calling 'The King of Western Bop'."

Because of all the hysteria in America, some of which had been reported in the UK, there were reservations in certain quarters about Elvis. Britain's foremost dance band leader, Jack Parnell, thought the record "tuneless", and the *Daily Mirror* denounced Elvis as a singer of "gut bucket music". The nation's teenagers, however, had other ideas, and following the lead of their contemporaries in America bought so many copies of "Heartbreak Hotel" that it remained in the top fifty listing for a record twenty-one weeks.

ELVIS PRESLEY

Colonel Parker now took the first steps towards easing the work-load that had been imposed on Elvis. One problem spot was the weekly trudge every Saturday from wherever he was to Shreveport for *Louisiana Hayride*, on which he had by now appeared over eighty times. This obligation played havoc with arrangements, not to mention putting a continuing strain on Elvis and his group. The show had now served its purpose in helping to get Elvis started, and the Colonel wanted out. The only trouble was that any buy-out of the long-term contract would cost Elvis – who was still by no means rich – nearly $1000 per month.

The Colonel had to take a gamble on Elvis being able to earn considerably more if he was free of *Hayride*, and so agreed to buy the contract back for a fee of $10,000 plus an agreement that the singer would play one more special concert on 31 March. This he did – and drew a capacity crowd of teenagers who screamed their approval at his songs and moaned their disappointment that he would not be returning to Shreveport. Just watching those kids and realizing how typical they were of others throughout the nation, the Colonel must then have known – if he had ever doubted – that his gamble was really no gamble at all.

During Elvis' visits to New York for *Stage Show*, RCA had taken the opportunity to have him record eight more songs in their plush and well-equipped downtown Manhattan studios. For these sessions, the line-up was trimmed again to just Elvis, Scotty, Bill and D.J. and a session piano player named Shorty Long. Gone were the extra guitar and backing group. Each and every number was delivered with great power by Elvis as pure rock 'n' roll, and their titles stand today as almost a hit parade of the greatest rock numbers. There was Carl Perkins' "Blue Suede Shoes"; two tributes to Arthur Crudup – "My Baby Left Me" and "So Glad You're Mine"; Bill Campbell's country-originated "One-Sided Love Affair"; "I'm Gonna Sit Right Down and Cry" written by Thomas Briggs; "Tutti Frutti", earlier a smash hit for its composer, Little Richard; "Lawdy Miss Clawdy", another revival of a hit record by Lloyd Price; and Jesse Stone's "Shake, Rattle and Roll", recorded by both the great blues singer Joe Turner, and Bill Haley and the Comets.

There are those who claim that these sessions and the earlier ones in Nashville gave the world Elvis at his very best – that neither he, nor any

Elvis signing his first film contract with Hal Wallis in Hollywood in 1956.

other rock artist for that matter, has ever quite matched them. Be that as it may, at that moment in history Elvis Presley had recorded enough unique and brilliant material to assure him a place in pop music history even if he never went into a recording studio again. That he did do so, over and over again, adding still more gems to the treasure trove of his work that is still played and enjoyed today, is the icing on the cake.

As Elvis had now proved himself as both a live performer and hit record maker, the next obvious step for Colonel Parker to take was to get him into the movies. Indeed, there had already been one or two tentative enquiries made to the Colonel's offices from Hollywood, and so on 1 April he and Elvis flew to film city to discuss a possible movie contract.

The man they went to see was producer Hal Wallis of Paramount Pictures, a prolific maker of feature films aimed at catching new public fads or featuring new media stars. He had seen Elvis' appearances on the television on the Dorseys' *Stage Show* and read in the press just what a stir the young singer was making among teenagers. And it was this newly affluent generation that Wallis saw as the audience for any movies he might make with Elvis Presley.

Elvis always wanted to play the gun-slinger Billy the Kid when he became a film star.

Wallis immediately put Elvis before the cameras and had him act a number of scenes which ranged in emotion from tenderness to the edge of violence. To appear with him Wallis brought in a veteran actor named Frank Faylen, who was to reflect later in his life that he was more famous for having made that screen test with Elvis than for any feature picture in which he appeared! Frank admitted, none the less, that he was impressed by Elvis' natural acting ability and was never in any doubt that the studio would want to use the youngster as long as they could find a suitable vehicle for him.

Colonel Parker was anxious to make a deal to get Elvis into films and for once did not haggle for long over a three-picture contract for which the singer would have a starting salary of $100,000. If the first movie was a success, his fee would then increase by $50,000 for each of the remaining two films.

For Elvis it was another dream come true, something he had never thought would happen to him. Talking about his trip to Hollywood, when he was on tour a week later, he said:

33-5-46

66   I took this screen test where I came in and was real happy and jolly and I didn't like it. And then I did this other one where I was mad at this guy and I liked that better – it was me. Mr Wallis asked me what kind of part I'd like, and I told him one like myself so I wouldn't have to do any excess acting. So he's having somebody write one for me like that.   99

One idea Elvis said he hoped to do was a film about Billy the Kid. "I love western films," he explained. "I've watched some of them dozens of times. I know the Billy the Kid story has been done before, but this time it will be real different. I won't sing, I want to be an actor. A real good one."

The stars of *Love Me Tender*, Richard Egan, Debra Paget and Elvis.

Rare photograph of Elvis in his screen test for his first film, *Love Me Tender*, which was then known as "The Reno Brothers".

Script conference during the making of *Love Me Tender*.

141

In fact, of course, the first film that Elvis made that summer was *Love Me Tender* (originally entitled *The Reno Brothers*), in which he co-starred with Richard Egan and Debra Paget, as the young brother left behind during the Civil War and tragically killed by his returning older brother who believes him to have stolen his girl. Elvis' death at the end of the picture, and his moving rendition of the title ballad, brought tears to the eyes of millions of his fans. It also demonstrated that he could act when given the opportunity, and the thirty or so pictures he made during the rest of his life – some good, some bad and a few really

Two publicity photographs of Elvis in *Love Me Tender*.

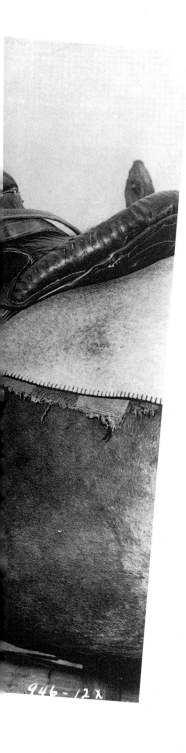

946 - 12 X

dreadful – showed that he had the talent to overcome the most banal script and ridiculous situation. The best of his movies truly comprise another jewel in his crown.

It was, in fact, in this same month that Elvis was first labelled the "King of Rock 'n' Roll". It happened in a colourful little article written on 19 April by Bea Ramirez, a fashionable young writer on a Texas newspaper, the *Waco News-Tribune*. After meeting with Elvis in the city, Miss Ramirez opened her story:

Elvis with fans on
the set of *Love
Me Tender*.

66   Shortly before he was to go on stage at the Heart O' Texas Coliseum, Elvis Presley, the new 21-year-old king of the rock 'n' roll set, sat in a darkened Cadillac limousine for an interview – well hidden from the sight of 4000 screaming, squealing teenagers who were on hand to welcome him on Tuesday night. All the hep cats were there and not enough fuzz [cops].   99

Though the article added little to what was already known about the singer – it was more full of wise-cracks made by Elvis than actual information – it was a clear indication of Elvis' new-found status and a pointer that his days of freedom were rapidly drawing to a close. Within a few months, in fact, Elvis would become a prisoner of his own fame – and remain so for the rest of his life, being either rushed to and from concerts in high-speed luxury cars, confined behind the well-guarded doors of hotel suites, or else hidden inside the high walls of his Memphis home, "Graceland". Soon, very soon, the days of travelling the open road with Scotty, Bill and D.J., stopping where and when the guys chose, would be no more than a memory.

Elvis looking somewhat isolated, giving a press conference in Oakland, California. (*Left*) Talking to Bea Ramirez, the Texan reporter who called him "the new 21-year-old king of the rock 'n' roll set" when he appeared in Texas in April 1956. (*Top*) A 1956 advertisement proclaiming the arrival of "The King".

"HEARTBREAK HOTEL • LONG, TALL SALLY • BLUE SUEDE SHOES"

THE KING IS COMING IN PERSON!

Elvis Presley

ONE DAY ONLY • 3 Performances • FRIDAY MAY 25

All Seats $1.50
Now On Sale

Fox THEATRE
Information
WO 3-7700

147

By 1956, Elvis was becoming a prisoner of his extraordinary fame.

April also brought Elvis another major television triumph. On 3 April
he appeared on the networked entertainment programme *The Milton
Berle Show*, which attracted an estimated audience of forty million – an
astonishing one in four people in the United States. The show,
broadcast from the aircraft carrier USS *Hancock* in dock at San Diego,
gave another pointer to Elvis' future – for the live audience consisted
almost entirely of sailors and their wives. The tremendous reception
that this older audience gave him was the first clear indication that Elvis
could attract wider groups than just teenagers. Despite what some critics
were saying about the limitations of his appeal and the possibility that
he might be only a passing fancy, Elvis demonstrated on that day that he
had the ability to captivate and entertain adults, too.

In that same month, Elvis made his debut at Las Vegas, the ritzy
gambling capital of America to which the world's great entertainers
were brought at fabulous expense to entertain those who were being
irresistibly parted from their money. Extraordinarily for someone who

**Elvis on the set of his second major TV
series with Milton Berle.**

***Opposite:* Elvis in Las Vegas before his first
series of night-club concerts in 1956.**

was at that time carrying all before him in theatres and auditoriums across the nation, Elvis' two-week run of appearances which began on 23 April was not a success.

May Mann, the show-business columnist who later became Elvis' friend, saw this Vegas debut and later gave an explanation for its failure.

66   Elvis was signed for Las Vegas by Sammy Lewis, the enterprising producer of the New Frontier Hotel. This was his first appearance in a plush Vegas night club, and his only one until 1969. Lewis signed Elvis for two weeks at $7500 per week. Sheckey Greene the comedian was second on the bill. A sign of Elvis' figure, fifty-feet high, was put out in front in blazing lights. But Danny Thomas and other well-known entertainers easily outdrew Elvis, the newcomer, who was not then quite ripe for Las Vegas' sophisticated older audiences. 99

Above: **Another revealing photograph of Elvis in Las Vegas just prior to his opening night.**

ELVIS A MILLIONAIRE IN 1 YEAR

MOSE, SWELLS RECORD TAKE

By MIKE KAPLAN

Hollywood, Oct. 23.
Controversy has always meant cash in show business and the latest proof is Elvis Presley, whose jet-propelled career will reach stratospheric heights in his first full year in the bigtime with an indicated gross income of at least $1,000,000. Tally is an underestimation, based on what he has done in the first nine months of 1956.

Despite the carping critics who contend he can't last, reasonable projections of future income indicate he'll do at least as well in 1957, with the tally possibly bouncing even higher as result of his share of an unprecedented $40,000,000 retail sales volume of Elvis Presley merchandise during the next 15 months.

Presley's entry into the bigtime usually is dated from his appearance on the Milton Berle show last midsummer. Actually, he had been a rising performer for some months prior to that as witness hefty disk sales and personal appearances that drew door-busting crowds.

Since the Berle show, however, Presley has been a true atomic-age phenomenon.

Estimate of $1,000,000 for his 1956 earnings is based solely on the known factors, which include unprecedented heights in some departments. The near-1,000,000 advance sale of his "Love Me Tender" disking for RCA Victor is an indication of the pace of his platters. For the 1956 calendar year, Presley figures to wind up with a total of at least 10,000,000 records sold. Figure represents a royalty return to him of about $450,000. Add to that an estimated $250,000 in picture deals, including the reported $100,000 for "Love Me Tender" (20th-Fox) as well as advances on his deal with Hal Wallis, and probably another $100,000 in television guest stints. Then, there are the personal appearances, about 40 in all by the end of the year, on which Presley's percentages vary but which are figured to total at least $200,000. There's $1,100,000 right there, plus returns from his music publishing firm.

Few of the actual Presley figures are available since his manager, Col. Tom Parker, is an astute and close-mouthed guide. Nor is there any concrete indication of the 1956 take on the merchandise tieups, which are figured to be considerable.

Any way it's figured, it's a safe bet that Presley's earnings for the 1956 and 1957 years will top $2,500,000.

The experience was not all bad for Elvis, however. He had worked long and hard for his success, and he was not about to give up on an audience now. So for those two weeks he gave it all he had, and although there were no hysterical outbursts, his raunchy style and sexy good looks certainly moved a good many of the women in a way they had not felt since the days of *their* teenage idol, Frank Sinatra.

As history shows, when Elvis returned to Las Vegas in 1969 he was older, wiser, if anything even more handsome, and now had all the stagecraft and musical skill necessary to enthrall totally even the most sceptical audiences. Many, in fact, fell under his spell in just the ecstatic way that his earliest teenage fans had done! Indeed, some of them *were* those same fans, now grown to maturity. And in the years which followed he repeatedly proved himself the biggest draw the gambling city had, and still has, ever seen.

By the summer of 1956, two years on from the fateful day when Elvis had got together with Scotty and Bill and recorded the epoch-making "That's All Right, Mama", he could look back on having proved himself in the areas which were to form the backbone of the rest of his career. He was a master of the live performance, a maker of internationally successful records, and a film star. His days on the road were over – super-stardom beckoned to the man whom a generation of teenagers would call "The King" and revere for the rest of his days, and beyond. The cost to him, though, was to be any kind of normal life and, ultimately, a sad and isolated death in 1977 amidst all the rich trappings that his rare talent brought him.

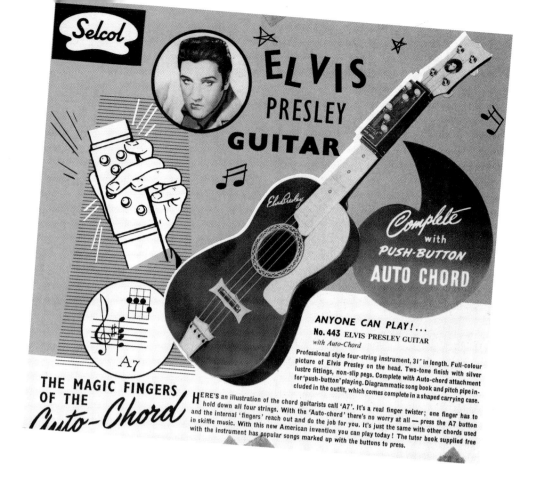

The magic fingers of the Auto-Chord

Here's an illustration of the chord guitarists call 'A7'. It's a real finger twister; one finger has to hold down all four strings. With the 'Auto-chord' there's no worry at all — press the A7 button and the internal 'fingers' reach out and do the job for you. It's just the same with other chords used in skiffle music. With this new American invention you can play today! The tutor book supplied free with the instrument has popular songs marked up with the buttons to press.

ANYONE CAN PLAY!...
No. 443 ELVIS PRESLEY GUITAR
with Auto-Chord

Professional style four-string instrument, 31" in length. Full-colour picture of Elvis Presley on the head. Two-tone finish with silver lustre fittings, non-slip pegs. Complete with Auto-chord attachment for 'push-button' playing. Diagrammatic song book and pitch pipe included in the outfit, which comes complete in a shaped carrying case.

An "Elvis Presley Guitar" – an early example of what was to become a flood of Presley merchandising.

The measure of his achievements can, of course, be judged by the fact that more than ten years after his death his name is still as familiar as ever and the interest in his records and films – not to mention his life – continues at an astonishingly high level. There is, perhaps, no one person better qualified to write Elvis' epitaph than the man who first sensed his latent talent and started him on the road to stardom. Sam Phillips still lives and works in Memphis pursuing his dream of finding and promoting new talent. He knew Elvis perhaps as well as anyone and also his contribution to modern music, and he has spoken about both with genuine warmth and conviction. First, the man himself.

" I really wish more people could have known Elvis as a person. I got to know where he was coming from, and the guy was much, much deeper and much more of a spiritual man than a lot of us may have thought.

The thing about his kind of success is that it's a vicious circle. You start out and you're so proud of your success and you say. 'God, I'll do anything to stay on top.' And then you find yourself saying, 'Well, gosh,

Opposite: Front-page story from *Variety*, 23 October 1956.

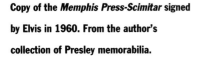

Copy of the *Memphis Press-Scimitar* signed by Elvis in 1960. From the author's collection of Presley memorabilia.

I know it's got to be over before too long and I've got to keep up this image. I'm very mortal, but I can't let the people know I'm mortal.' But there's just no such thing as being an island unto yourself.

I believe he needed help from the standpoint of forgetting the damn money and forgetting the damn fame. I'm not putting anybody down, but I'm sure that after a time, Elvis felt like he didn't know how to do that. He was closed off from the pleasures of everyday life.

He needed more than anybody I've ever seen in my life to have been able to throw away the whole damn book, in his home town at least, and do what he damn well pleased. I feel as fervently as I have ever felt anything that he would have been alive today if that had happened. **99**

And of Elvis' music, Sam has this to say:

66 His contributions to the great voids that existed during the 'fifties for a different approach to music for young people were monumental. No doubt he was the catalyst to the 'sticking power' of this form of music that truly changed the approaches to music by making it 'freer' and less pretentious for the whole world.

With the likes of Carl Perkins, Johnny Cash and Jerry Lee Lewis and the many great black artists, he helped pave a solid footing for all aspiring young artists to spring from. His feel for white and black country blues, along with his love for fundamental religious music, will stand him right at the top forever in the history of the basic changes that were so needed during this era of our music culture. These changes made life more meaningful and honest for us all and we are all in his debt for the past, the present and the future. 99

"Elvis helped pave a solid footing for all aspiring young artists to spring from" – Sam Phillips.

elvis on record A DISCOGRAPHY
1954–1956

These are the records that Elvis released during the years on the road to stardom from 1954 to 1956. Copies of the original discs are now of the utmost rarity, and surviving examples of the first five Sun records are worth well in excess of $250 each. The tracks Elvis cut for Sam Phillips are all now available on a single album, *The Complete Sun Sessions*, while the early records he made for RCA can also be found on the album *Elvis Presley*.

SUN SESSIONS

1954

That's All Right, Mama (Arthur Crudup)

(B side) Blue Moon of Kentucky (Bill Monroe)

SUN 209. Released: August 1954

Good Rockin' Tonight (Roy Brown)

(B side) I Don't Care if the Sun Don't Shine (Mack David)

SUN 210. Released: October 1954

1955

Milkcow Blues Boogie (Kokomo Arnold)

(B side) You're a Heartbreaker (Jack Sallee)

SUN 215. Released: January 1955

I'm Left, You're Right, She's Gone (Stanley Kessler)

(B side) Baby, Let's Play House (Arthur Gunter)

SUN 217. Released: May 1955

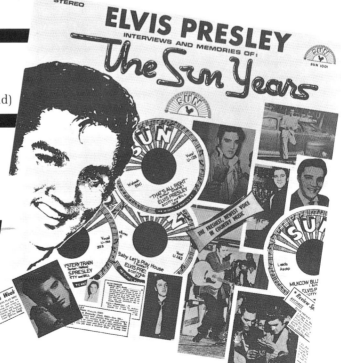

Elvis and his musicians taking a break during an early recording session.

Mystery Train (Junior Parker and Sam Phillips)

(B side) I Forgot to Remember to Forget (Stanley Kessler and Charlie Feathers)

SUN 223. Released: August 1955

RCA–VICTOR SESSIONS

1956

Heartbreak Hotel (Mae Boren Axton)

(B side) I Was the One (Aaron Schroeder, Hal Blair and Claude Demetrius)

RCA 6420. Released: January 1956

I Want You, I Need You, I Love You (Maurice Mysels and Ira Kosloff)

(B side) My Baby Left Me (Arthur Crudup)

RCA 6540. Released: May 1956

Hound Dog (Jerry Lieber and Mike Stoller)

(B side) Don't Be Cruel (Otis Blackwell)

RCA 6604. Released: July 1956

Blue Suede Shoes (Carl Perkins)

(B side) Tutti-Frutti (Richard Penniman and Dorothy La Bostrie)

RCA 6636. Released: September 1956

I'm Counting on You (Don Robertson)

(B side) I Got a Woman (Ray Charles)

RCA 6637. Released: September 1956

A much sought-after souvenir of Elvis' first records for Sun.

The legendary artist at work doing what he did best – singing.

An RCA commemorative album of Elvis' first sessions for the company.

I'll Never Let You Go (Jimmy Wakely)

(B side) I'm Gonna Sit Right Down and Cry over You (Thomas Briggs)

RCA 6638. Released: September 1956

Tryin' to Get to You (Margie Singleton and Rose Marie McCoy)

(B side) I Love You Because (Leon Payne)

RCA 6639. Released: September 1956

Blue Moon (Lorenz Hart and Richard Rodgers)

(B side) Just Because (Bob Shelton, Joe Shelton and Sid Robin)

RCA 6640. Released: September 1956

Money Honey (Jesse Stone)

(B side) One-Sided Love Affair (Bill Campbell)

RCA 6641. Released: September 1956

Shake, Rattle and Roll (Charles Calhoun)

(B side) Lawdy, Miss Clawdy (Lloyd Price)

RCA 6642. Released: September 1956

Love Me Tender (Ken Darby)

(B side) Any Way You Want Me (Aaron Schroeder and Cliff Owens)

RCA 6643. Released: September 1956